INDIE AUTHOR MAGAZINE

HELLO AND WELCOME!

I'm Indie Annie, and I'm thrilled you're reading this gorgeous full-color version of IAM. Did you know that you can also access all the information, education, and inspiration in our app? It's available on both the iOS App Store and Google Play. And for those that prefer to listen to me read articles, you can pop over to Spotify or our website. Happy Reading!

X

IndieAuthorMagazine.com

Download on the
App Store

GET IT ON
Google Play

Spotify

LAUNCH STRATEGIES

ON THE COVER

INDIE AUTHOR MAGAZINE

PUBLISHER
Chelle Honiker

CREATIVE DIRECTOR
Alice Briggs

MANAGING EDITOR
Robyn Sarty

WRITERS
Angela Archer
Elaine Bateman
Patricia Carr
Laurel Decher
Fatima Fayez
Gill Fernley
Greg Fishbone

WRITERS
Remy Flagg
Chrishaun Keller Hanna
Jac Harmon
Marion Hermannsen
Monica Leonelle
Kasia Lasinska
Bre Lockhart
Anne Lown
Sìne Màiri MacDougall
Merri Maywether
Lasairiona McMaster
Susan Odev
Nicole Schroeder
Emilia Zeeland

PUBLISHER
Athenia Creative
6820 Apus Dr.
Sparks, NV, 89436 USA
775.298.1925

ISSN 2768-7880 (online)–ISSN 2768-7872 (print)

From the Publisher

DROWNING IN A SEA OF DISTRACTIONS

Like many creatives, I suffer from a terminal case of bright shiny object syndrome. I see ideas everywhere, and run after them like a puppy chasing a ball, leaving old ones by the wayside.

I've also developed the terrible habit of stopping (too) often to check email, social media notifications, or reply to text messages.

Adding to the mix is the endless noise of technology interruptions. The stream of notifications from eight devices beep, ding, and chime so often they've lost their purpose. I ignore them.

Then I wonder why my word count is disastrously low and the task list remains unfinished.

Allow me to sum up this predicament in our new modern shared language, a relatable meme:

Metaphorically speaking, I've lost control of the day.

Taking Control Again

I've made my sacred project list. No more detours, however bright and shiny. I'm shutting off notifications and committing to completely focus on one thing until it's finished.

I'm also thinking of having this quote discretely tattooed somewhere I'll see it often:

> Rachel Johanna Strodel
> @RJStrodel
>
> easily the most relatable email I've received
>
> ~~————————————~~
>
> **need to postpone**
> Hi Rachel, I have lost control of the day.

> "Concentrate all your thoughts upon the work at hand.
> The sun's rays do not burn until brought to a focus."
> Alexander Graham Bell

Focus. That's my word for 2022.

This issue offers multiple solutions and suggestions for helping you regain control of your day. As you navigate your plan for a new year, I'd like to ask that you share your ideas with me. We're starting a project to leverage the "wisdom in the room" from our readers. Drop me an email and let me know your thoughts.

To Your Success,
Chelle
Publisher
Indie Author Magazine

From the Managing Editor

"You can never cross the ocean until you have the courage to lose sight of the shore."–Christopher Columbus

January is a month for fresh starts and looking forward to a year full of exciting possibilities. We've made our goals; we've set our plans in place. Now it's time to put them into action.

Hopefully, your plan for the new year includes heaps of new books. (For me, "heaps" means two. That's where I'm at in my career. Heaps for you could mean twenty or anywhere in between.) But writing those books is only part of the equation. We need to give our book the best send-off possible.

Whether you want to try the rapid release model, navigate the wonders of taking your book wide to all retailers, or plan on giving your book a big, splashy release, we've got you covered this month. And if you need some extra motivation, check out the featured author interview with the ever-inspiring Elana Johnson.

For me, 2022 is going to look a lot different than last year. I'm stepping down as managing editor for *Indie Author Magazine*. It has been an amazing experience, watching this little idea become an incredible concept that the indie author world has embraced. Each month, the writers have impressed me with their talent and the heart they've put into their articles. But it's time for me to cross my ocean, to focus on my writing. It's scary, out where the waves dwarf my little ship, but I'm ready.

No matter what you've got planned for the new year, don't let fear be the thing that stops you from achieving it. Because you are more than that fear, and I believe you are capable of letting go of the shoreline.

Robyn Sarty
Managing Editor,
Indie Author Magazine

SUBSTACK FOR AUTHORS

What do authors Salman Rushdie and Chuck Palahniuk have in common with a small army of indie authors? They're actively publishing newsletters and creative content on the newsletter platform Substack.

Let's look at why this new platform might be the hottest place to publish your next novel and connect with a whole new group of fans.

WHAT IS SUBSTACK?

At its most basic, Substack is a newsletter platform. Founded in 2017 by Chris Best, Jairaj Sethi, and Hamish McKenzie, as of August 2021, Substack had more than 250,000 paying subscribers. It's attracted a variety of content creators, including journalists, comic artists, religion writers, and political commentators.

Substack is free to use, regardless of newsletter size. It also offers creators the option of setting up paid subscriptions to earn money on their content. The only time Substack gets paid is when someone subscribes to a paid newsletter, as a percentage of those subscriptions goes back to the company.

Most people use their Substack as both a newsletter and as a blog because all content is archived at a permanent URL on a writer's Substack page. If someone subscribes today, they can easily go back and read everything a writer has written in the past.

The Substack interface is also dead simple. Unlike most newsletter platforms, there's no need to design multiple

> " Most people use their Substack as both a newsletter and as a blog. "

> **Indie authors are using Substack as a way to not only keep in touch with their readers but share a bit more about themselves, their writing process, or some of their shorter fictional pieces.**

templates or layouts. Although there's a little work involved in starting a new Substack, once you get past the setup phase, sending out new newsletters is as easy as drinking that first cup of coffee in the morning.

It's important to note that Substack is about content, not business. While it's great to share content, it's not a good choice for people who need advanced newsletter capabilities. Automation, such as onboarding email sequences, isn't possible. You also can't have multiple templates for different audiences or purposes. And although you can segment newsletters between free and paid, that's about as far as segmentation goes.

HOW AUTHORS ARE USING SUBSTACK NOW

As a relatively new platform, people are still learning what it can do.

Some authors are experimenting with it as an alternative publishing platform. Looking at it as one part Wattpad, one part Patreon, they're publishing short stories and novels in serial form. On Palahniuk's Substack (https://chuckpalahniuk.substack.com/) he's publishing his novel *Greener Pastures* in fifty-two installments, while Rushdie (https://salmanrushdie.substack.com/) is publishing a work entitled *Seventh Wave*. Both novels are available only for paid subscribers, but both offer preview chapters as well as other content for free.

But Substack isn't just for big names in the traditional publishing world. Author Patrick E. McLean (https://patrickem-clean.substack.com/) moved his mailing list to Substack in June. His paid subscribers gain access to his How to Succeed in Evil

> "It's really simple to send out a newsletter that's readable and has a website-end that can be organized like a mini-publication."
> Jon Auerbach

series as a membership reward. He's also shared some of his other work, including a novella entitled *Beowulf and the Dragon*, as both written stories and audio files.

Another indie author, Elle Griffin (https://ellegriffin.substack.com/) is currently serializing her gothic novel *Obscurity* on Substack, and giving her paid readers exclusive access to a Discord group. Meanwhile, Jon Auerbach (https://jonauerbach.substack.com/) is serializing his *Guild of Magic* and *Guild of Tokens* fantasy novels there for both paid and free subscribers.

Other indie authors are keeping their novels on KDP, Vella, or other platforms, but are using Substack as a way to not only keep in touch with their readers but share a bit more about themselves, their writing process, or some of their shorter fictional pieces.

WHY YOU MIGHT CONSIDER IT FOR YOUR OWN WORK

Some people came to Substack as a replacement for a previous mailing list platform. The fact that it's free is one attraction, but more than that, it offers a cleaner interface that focuses on the craft of writing. Auerbach chose Substack because "it's really simple to send out a newsletter that's readable and has a website-end that can be organized like a mini-publication."

Others like it because, in addition to a free newsletter, it's possible to charge an annual subscription, bringing in a decent income stream even for new authors. The simplicity of the platform makes it more conducive to publishing long-form content. Some authors use sites like Royal Road or Wattpad to serialize

> **Shaiyan Khan from Substack's partnership team explains that the platform can be a great fit for authors because it makes it simple to build a relationship with their audience.**

their stories, but then have to resort to asking for donations on PayPal or setting up a Patreon in order to earn anything from their work.

Shaiyan Khan from Substack's partnership team explains that the platform can be a great fit for authors because it makes it simple to build a relationship with their audience. "By providing authors with the tools and services they need to succeed," Khan says, "we're freeing them to focus on the hard part: the writing."

Sci-fi and fantasy author Alex S. Garcia (https://xenin. substack.com/) agrees. He chose Substack because the monetizing system "is in-built, rather than relying on something external like Patreon." And Auerbach's a fan of the paid option because it "makes it easier for me to focus on providing value to all of my paid subscribers, with enough flexibility to offer higher-end items for annual/founder tier subscribers."

THE COMMUNITY

One of the biggest reasons people like Substack has nothing to do with the technical elements or the pricing. Unlike traditional email platforms and trendy content sites, there is a vibrant and growing community of Substack users.

The growth of the community is something Substack itself is working actively to promote. As Khan says, "being independent shouldn't mean being alone." The Substack Community Team hosts weekly question and shoutout threads, and the company

> **Is Substack right for you? It depends on your goals and how you want to approach your publishing future.**

Jackie Dana

Jackie Dana is a freelance writer and author living in St. Louis, MO. She writes Story Cauldron on Substack (story-cauldron.substack.com), where she ponders storytelling and writing topics as well as publishes her YA fantasy series The Favor Faeries.

also sponsors free programs like Substack Grow that bring together smaller content producers to discuss how to improve their newsletters while getting to know each other. Recently they have branched out into online and in-person user meetups.

Outside of Substack, there are Facebook groups and Discord servers that help connect the community as well. One of the biggest is Griffin's "Substack Writers Unite" Discord group (https://discord.gg/q9S4feaDVz) that brings together both fiction and nonfiction writers to discuss everything from craft to audience building to going paid.

Is Substack right for you? It depends on your goals and how you want to approach your publishing future. As Khan points out, it's a different kind of publishing that allows authors to "take their readers on a journey while writing, growing an audience and interacting with readers the whole while, instead of working on a book in isolation and releasing a static work at one point in time." And for many of us, making those connections along the way makes Substack a worthy alternative to standard indie publishing. ◼

Jackie Dana

Dear Indie Annie,

I know I need to run ads if I want to grow my revenue, but all the numbers are making my brain hurt. ACOS, CPC, Impressions, CTR: I am trying to keep them straight, but all the acronyms and calculations are confusing me. I can't remember what the letters stand for or what the terms mean, and the numbers keep jumping around. Please help!

Innumerate in Indiana

Oh, my sweet, darling Innumerate in Indiana,

I feel your pain. I really do. When the exceptional team here at IAM passed your question to me, I hid in my bedroom for a week, and they had to entice me out with an offer of iced cinnamon buns and whiskey-laced hot chocolate with gold-dusted marshmallows.

Even then, I begged them to give me a different question. Advertising jargon makes my blood run as cold as an evening stroll on Mercury. Sadly, understanding this alien language is essential if you wish to grow your sales. And as much as we are all in this business because we love storytelling, the reason you and many others are here reading this glorious publication is that you want or need to make money from your art.

So what advice can I give you, my friend?

Take the time to learn how to run ads and apply the techniques or find someone else who can do it for you.

Sorry for being so blunt. We all face this dilemma. Like that wonderful children's story *We're Going on a Bear Hunt* by Michael Rosen, we can't go over it. We can't go under it. We have to go through it.

And we *all* have to go through it. Sales do not magically happen. Mastering the dark arts of advertising is essential if you are serious about making any income from your books.

Like any new skill, at first, the terms are hard to grasp. I'll let you in on a little secret. When I emerged from my cocoon, I had to look up all the acronyms, and I do this every time I run a campaign. They just don't stick in my head, but what does stick is how valuable they are to analyzing the success of a campaign.

Let's quickly run through some simple definitions.

Need help from your favorite Indie Aunt?
Ask Dear Indie Annie a question at
IndieAnnie@indieauthormagazine.com

ACoS (Advertising Cost of Sale) is a percentage showing how much a sale costs you in advertising money, calculated by dividing total ad spend by total sales.

CPC (Cost per Click) is the amount you, the seller, pays when a buyer clicks on your ad.

CTR (Click Through Rate) is the number of potential buyers who viewed (impressions) and then clicked on your ads.

Impressions have nothing to do with the roasting of public figures on *Saturday Night Live*. Impressions mean the number of times prospective buyers have seen your ad.

The trick is to get the ad in front of people who are not only interested enough to click through to the sales page but who will also buy your book once they get there. Metrics help you understand how well that is happening and where in the process you may be losing people.

For example, if your CTR is low, then the problem may lie with your keywords, your cover, ad copy, etc. In short, the advertising is not attracting potential buyers to your book. If you have a good CTR but low sales, then look at your blurb, what can be seen in the "Look inside" feature, etc.

It is worth investing the time into understanding the language of advertising and what it can tell you about your book's appeal and your marketing strategy. The trick is to test variations until you find winning formulas: ads that convert from impressions through clicks to sales. Initially, making a sale and increasing those sales are important so you can gather useful data. Later, you can explore the profitability of the ad, i.e., is the CPC too high? In short, which ads make the most profit?

If all this is making you want to disappear under your bed sheets and never write another word, think about hiring someone to do it for you or perhaps trade skills with another writer who is skilled with ads but who can't afford an editor and so on.

Some people prefer the science of advertising to the wizardry of words. Reach out and find these precious souls or learn how to weave the magic yourself. And if you crack the code, call me.

Happy Writing,
Indie Annie

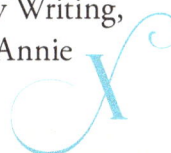

10 TIPS FOR
KICKSTARTER

Simply put, Kickstarter is a crowdfunding platform. For those wondering what that means, crowdfunding is the practice of funding a project by raising small amounts of money from a large number of people. If you're like many folks, your knowledge of the Kickstarter platform begins with that electronic cat accessory you almost backed and ends with a sweet-looking tabletop elf game your friend shared a link for in 2019.

But Kickstarter is not just for gadgets, games, and gizmos. No, sir. Kickstarter has a thriving community of artists with global projects in just about any medium, books included.

In fact, across the top of the Kickstarter main page are eight categories, the last of which is "Publishing." Based on that information alone, one could reasonably infer that authors are finding some measure of success there. Whether this particular path is on your individual roadmap, we can't say, but here's ten tips for using Kickstarter to help you decide.

1 **Do Your Research:** Review campaigns similar to what you'd like to create. What do they have in common? Is every campaign giving out a pin or signed books? Does each tier include an additional digital item or something else?

Most importantly, is your project a good fit for Kickstarter? Not all ideas work on a crowdfunding platform. If you are struggling to find any comparable projects that have seen success, there might be a reason for that.

You should absolutely have an idea of how campaigns related to your future projects look, work, and perform before starting. In the interest of honesty, your first campaign probably won't make a ton of money, but like books you publish after number one, you get better with each new endeavor. Research, organization, and realistic expectations are invaluable.

② **Polish Your Pitch:** In videos and on the page, use clear messaging, don't ramble, and be professional. Kickstarter backers, like readers, can get bored or uninterested if the campaign pages are overly wordy, lack specific or attention-grabbing details, and generally don't use strong copywriting. Remember to make a solid, well-thought-out video for the story, aka sales page. The video and corresponding sales copy is your chance to pitch your project, not sell yourself. You should be answering the question, "Why would someone want to buy/back this?" in the most interesting and concise way possible.

Pro Tip: Learn about copywriting. Many books and courses are available to help authors hone the skill of copywriting, something you will find a multitude of uses for during your author career.

Lean into the Differences: What does your book or project have that is different or sets your project apart?

③ If it is nonfiction, is there a thought-provoking personal story behind it? If it is fiction, what can you capitalize on that's really quirky (i.e. distinctive alien species, vibrant setting, eccentric characters)? Within reason, don't be afraid to emphasize the unique bits and pieces of your creative work. Readers and backers want to find something new and exciting. It's your job to figure out what that is in relation to your project.

The Imagery and Messaging Should Fit: Images and words are sales tools. Are you trying to publish

④ a Dark Romance book? Use the copy and imagery to really drop the backer into the Dark Romance vibe: darker colors, grittier keywords, etc. Think of the imagery and messaging as part of the branding.

Pro Tip: Certain colors evoke certain emotions; this is called color psychology and can be used effectively to help consumers *feel* a certain way about a product or, in this case, a Kickstarter project.

⑤ **Use Tools to Help:** Kickstarter has an entire resource section of free information, but they also offer paid options. One example of a tool that might be worth the cost is BackerKit. com, a crowdfunding management and fulfillment software platform that helps creators streamline surveys, add-ons, delivery of items, and more. Tools like BackerKit often have browser integrations for ease of use and can save you time, effort, and potentially cost in the long run.

⑥ **Rules Are Not Meant to Be Broken:** Kickstarter's rules are not suggestions but a set of terms that creators agree to when creating their projects. If you like the Kickstarter platform and want to continue to use it, take five minutes to read the "Our Rules" section of the Kickstarter website. And before you worry about what type of legal jargon you're about to digest, it's only five main guidelines that will all seem fairly innocuous upon review.

7 Rewards Are Life: As mentioned in tip number one, give yourself a baseline by paying attention to what other campaigns offer as rewards. The sky is the limit with rewards but be sure that a) you can afford the cost to produce the reward and b) the reward is appropriate for the amount backed. Yes, your backers will love cool items, but a bank account in the red after a successful Kickstarter campaign kind of defeats the purpose.

8 Communicate with Backers Regularly: This includes checking in at specified dates and hitting all milestones, which is also a Kickstarter rule/expectation (see tip number six). The platform encourages updates, thank-you messages, stretch goals, and other communication as well.

9 Remember that Kickstarter *is* Marketing: This isn't a platform that works without effort (do those even exist?); you can't drop a new project in the queue with zero promotion and expect to find success. Sorry to say this, but you probably have to be social and put yourself and your project out there. If you approach any marketing without knowledge, commitment, or an interest in the project, you're facing an uphill climb.

As author and successful Kickstarter creator, Russell P. Nohelty said, "If you're not excited, the fans will not be excited. If you don't show them why they should buy, they're not going to buy."

Pro Tip: Always include call-to-action buttons and social media sharing links—a standard marketing guideline for any platform.

10 Don't Forget about Data: One of the most valuable benefits of Kickstarter is the data generated, everything from funding success rates overall to the performance of unsuccessful projects. You can even compare project dates with Facebook ads for a specified author (on Facebook) to see what type of advertising they ran.

To add another insight from Russell, "Even if you fail, you get data. If you succeed wildly, you get data. If you are somewhere in the middle, you get data…. As long as you are accumulating first-hand data, you'll be further ahead than you were yesterday."

Pro Tip: Kicktraq.com and BiggerCake.com are two more tools that can help with deciphering analytics, both before and after your campaign.

With the above tips in mind, go forth and create. Or at least research. Since its inception, Kickstarter has funded over two hundred thousand projects with over six billion dollars. What do you have to lose by looking into it?

Just as Kickstarter states on their Publishing category main page, now is the time to "Explore how writers and publishers are using Kickstarter to bring new literature, periodicals, podcasts, and more to life."

Many thanks to Russell P. Nohelty and Monica Leonelle for their assistance with this article. If you are looking for more information, check out their book Get Your Book Selling on Kickstarter: The Definitive Guide, *coming in mid-2022 after a successful Kickstarter campaign used to fund the project.* ■

Bre Lockhart

Get documents done anywhere

Now available for your Android & iOS mobile device

Dragon® Anywhere professional-grade mobile dictation makes it easy to create documents of any length, edit, format and share them directly from your mobile device-whether visiting clients, a job site, or your local coffee shop.

- ✓ Continuous dictation and no word limits
- ✓ 99% accurate with powerful voice editing and formatting
- ✓ Access customized words and auto-text across all devices
- ✓ Share documents by email, Dropbox, Evernote and more

Select a flexible pricing plan [**Subscribe now** ▾] *Credit Card Required. After your 7 day free trial, the monthly subscription begins at $15 per month. Cancel at anytime.

WriteLink.To/Dragon

MAKING A NAME FOR HERSELF

HOW ELANA JOHNSON—AND LIZ ISAACSON, JESSIE NEWTON, AND DONNA JEFFRIES—LEFT TRADITIONAL PUBLISHING TO INSPIRE INDIE SUCCESS

Over the fourteen years she's spent in the self-publishing industry, Elana Johnson has learned to use her strengths. The *USA Today* bestselling Romance and Women's Fiction author and CEO of AEJ Creative Works, Inc., knows how to compartmentalize, so even when her to-do list is a mile long, she can focus on what she's working on at the moment. She's an effective multitasker too, which comes in handy when she's working on multiple projects at once. And though she didn't realize it at first, she's a quick writer as well.

In fact, she's great at it. And even now that she has more than 160 titles to her name, she isn't planning on stopping anytime soon.

Well, technically, they're not all to her name—some of them are credited to Liz Isaacson, Jessie Newton, or Donna Jeffries instead, the pen names she uses in conjunction with her own. Each of her four author names focuses on a separate subgenre of Romance or Women's Fiction, and each is successful because of Johnson's effort and years of writing experience. But these days, she isn't keeping that knowledge to herself. Her Indie Inspiration with Elana Johnson Discussion Group on Facebook has more than 2,700 members in every stage of the publishing journey, from experienced indies to those just starting out.

"I've made a lot of mistakes and tried a lot of things that worked and didn't work," she says. "So I have a lot of experience, and my goal is to tell you about all of those—good, bad, ugly—so that you will feel inspired in your own career to make mistakes or to experiment or to step outside of the box that other people are saying you have to stay in."

> Each of her four author names focuses on a separate subgenre of Romance or Women's Fiction, and each is successful because of Johnson's effort and years of writing experience.

> "So I have a lot of experience, and my goal is to tell you about all of those—good, bad, ugly—so that you will feel inspired in your own career to make mistakes or to experiment or to step outside of the box that other people are saying you have to stay in."
> Elana Johnson

BREAKING FROM TRADITION

Johnson's path to self-publishing success started, quite literally, on a more traditional route. After finishing a Young Adult Dystopian novel in 2009, she began querying and landed a literary agent at the end of that year. Her manuscript sold to Simon & Schuster the next year and published a year later in 2011. But when she self-published a short story set in the same world as her novel, her mindset began to shift.

"That was my first experience with Amazon and KDP [Kindle Direct Publishing], where you can publish it yourself," Johnson says. "And I just remember... looking at that book cover in KDP and going, 'I want a lot of those. I want a lot more of those.'"

She stuck with traditional publishing long enough to complete her first book's trilogy, but the traditional publishing process wasn't quite what she'd envisioned. For one, it was exceedingly slow, and for another, finding a home for some of her other novels was becoming a chore. Still, when she decided to switch to self-publishing, she didn't have immediate smooth sailing.

"I don't know if you were around in 2014, but Chris Fox's *Write to Market* was not around," Johnson says. "All of the Facebook groups … where we find out a lot of the information and we learn self-publishing, they did not exist." She started with self-publishing her finished works that were passed over by traditional publishers, but they never sold well, and eventually, she decided to take them down. "Everybody will be grateful for that," she says with a laugh.

Her breakthrough started in 2014 when she decided to transition from the Sci-Fi genre into Romance. She published her first books in the genre, Contemporary Christian Cowboy Romances, under the pen name Liz Isaacson in 2015, and she found her calling in the publishing world. Three years later, Johnson cleaned up the titles published under her own name and rebranded herself as a

Contemporary Beach Romance author. In 2020, Jessie Newton was born as an author of Women's Fiction, and Donna Jeffries began publishing Romantic Comedies last year. These women are all technically Elana Johnson, but she refers to them as if they're separate individuals—and in some ways, that's the way she hopes readers view them too.

"I hope this doesn't sound super arrogant, but I already know a lot about launching and packaging and writing and marketing and advertising. I can't truly ever be new again," she says. "I can't erase that, but I can launch into a new genre as basically an unknown and see how it goes."

A WEALTH OF KNOWLEDGE, A SOURCE OF INSPIRATION

Alongside her Romance novels, Johnson also began publishing a series of writing and marketing guides, *Indie Inspiration for Self-Publishers*, in 2019. The books cover how to write cover copy, marketing systems, and methods for adjusting to a rapid release schedule, all skills she's incorporated in her own work. But it was the Facebook group the series spawned that, after the release of the series' third book in October 2020, took off in ways Johnson never expected. Nowadays, the Indie Inspiration with Elana Johnson Discussion Group has amassed more than 2,700 members, and it's still growing steadily each week.

"The group is an incredible source of information and inspiration for indie authors," writes April Wilson, a Contemporary Romance author who's been part of the Facebook group since May of last year. "Elana manages to keep the group very positive and focused on author inspiration. She's very active in the group and steers its direction herself."

When she first created the group, Johnson had worried her messages wouldn't resonate with members, especially when what she wrote contradicted what well-established authors were saying in other self-publishing groups. But she's found that many people agree with what she writes. Beyond that, she hopes her posts encourage authors to think outside the box and to not be afraid of making mistakes, just like she's learned to do over the years.

"I grew a lot when I finally was like, 'Enough. I'm tired of listening to all the fear statements and worrying so much about what I do and how it's going to be taken by others. I'm going to do what I think is best for me and my business,'" she says. "So that's my goal: to inspire people to think outside the box and to operate their businesses without any fear at all."

"I can launch into a new genre as basically an unknown and see how it goes."
Elana Johnson

REASON TO WRITE

Even now, Johnson admits she's surprised she can make a full-time living from her books. She has published three titles as Donna Jeffries, eleven titles as Jessie Newton, and fifty-four titles as herself—and that's not counting the Indie Inspiration series. And by the end of this year, Johnson will have published her hundredth title as Liz Isaacson. From a business standpoint, she could stop writing if she wanted to. A friend even asked her recently whether she had ever considered shifting from her role as an author to that of a publisher.

But she's come to realize that she doesn't want to give up storytelling. For her, the process of writing fiction is therapeutic. "It's a way to connect to other human beings who are going through the same hard things that I have to go through," she says. "It's almost a silent way of saying, 'Don't worry, I've got you. We're going to fix this by the end, and it's going to be okay.'"

She admits that just as surprising as her own success is that it won't always translate across books or authors—publishing methods that work for one person don't necessarily work for another, and even among her own books, some titles just don't sell as well.

Take her writing speed, for example. Johnson churns out words much faster than most—she finished her first published novel, the one that sold to Simon & Schuster, in just seventeen days. But even her newest pen names have seen plenty of success on their own without the massive backlog or years' worth of readers her Liz Isaacson or Elena Johnson titles have produced.

"I think often we think that—that somebody who writes fast is doing better than we are, or someone who releases more books than we are is somehow doing something better than we are, and that's not true," she says. "You just have to figure out what works for you and what fits your life, and that is what's best for you and what you should be doing." ■

Nicole Schroeder

> Her posts encourage authors to think outside the box and to not be afraid of making mistakes

Rapid Release to Rapid Riches?

RESOURCES

Johnson, Elana. *Writing and Releasing Rapidly: Indie Inspiration Volume One.*

Cooper, Mal. Cooper, Jill. *HELP! My Launch Plan Sucks.*

Martelle, Craig. *Release Strategies: Plan your self-publishing schedule for maximum benefit (Successful Indie Author Book 2)*

20Books Vegas 2021 Rapid Release Marketing.

Could rapidly releasing your books be the fastest way to financial success? Well, it might be one of them.

What is "rapid release"? The rapid release strategy is to publish each book quickly enough that the previous book in your series is still in its launch window, allowing you to take advantage of the extra visibility during the first thirty days of release. It sounds just like writing fast, doesn't it? Well, hold on to your hat, because there's so much more to it.

In her popular talk at the 20Booksto50k Vegas 2021 conference, Elana Johnson explained that rapid release is more than just writing and publishing quickly; it's about the processes that sit behind the books you produce. You have to be able to manage a launch schedule for each book.

In her successful book, *Writing and Releasing Rapidly*, Elana tells us to write fast, an estimated five to ten thousand words a day, in order to release a full-length novel every month, although it is also possible to queue books up for release. But there are other considerations; those books require covers. You need the resources to buy those covers or design them yourself, and they need to be edited. Editing one book can be expensive—can you afford to have three books edited before you receive any royalties from the first one? Can you find an editor who is available to work with your schedule? And don't forget the formatting! And finding speedy ARC readers.

Elana uses a mixture of soft, medium, and hard launches, each requiring a different amount of effort. The first and last books in a series would be launched hard with all the bells and whistles of ad campaigns, emails, newsletter swaps, and social media campaigns, while she would spend less time and attention on the others.

In the popular book, *HELP! My Launch Plan Sucks*, by Mal and Jill Cooper, Mal explains that at one point, she was writing a book a week but with only the bare essentials of marketing. It's important to her to keep enjoying what she's doing, which is, of course, another important component to success in writing. Mal says, "Releasing a book a week forever and always feeling like one's under the gun is not a great way to enjoy life. I was burning out."

Good news! You don't have to release *that* fast!

It is possible to line up books for release so you don't have to produce a book a month, but you do need to know how long it will take you to produce your novel. That includes everything from writing to launching and marketing.

MANAGING READER EXPECTATIONS

Writer and publisher Michael Anderle stresses that the most important consideration for someone thinking of trying to rapid release is "setting the expectations of your readers on what time frame you can really handle and deal with. If you are an eight-week-between-books person, then start that way and stay that way. It might suck in the beginning that sales go slow, but you won't regret it later when sales nosedive because fans have dropped you after missing your release."

Be honest with yourself about what you can deliver.

Author Craig Martelle recommends planning your release to broaden your reach and

"Rapid release is more than just writing and publishing quickly; it's about the processes that sit behind the books you produce."
Elana Johnson

increase sales. In his most successful series, he released ten books in ten months. His nonfiction book *Release Strategies* is another popular book that covers this subject. In it, Martelle lists the pros and cons of his personal experience of rapid releasing.

Pros:

- You will gain enhanced visibility from having two books on Amazon's New Release list at the same time.
- You will save money by running fewer ads.
- You will keep readers engaged.

Cons:

- You will need to do a lot of upfront work to manage the editing and creation of covers.
- Critics will question the quality of books without reading them.

CREATING *YOUR* RAPID RELEASE STRATEGY

Work through the following questions to determine if you can make use of rapid releasing and, if so, how. Once you've answered these questions, you'll be in a great position to know if you can make a go of it or, at least, work out what you need to do to prepare for a rapid release of your next series.

How quickly can you write month in and month out?

If you want to release a book every month, with a word count of sixty thousand words, you'll need to write two thousand words per day. Do you have time to do that? Can you write fast enough and keep up that pace? Have you ever recorded your word count per hour?

Do you need to build up a backlog of books in order to release one a month?

If you want to rapid release a six-book series, but your pace is about one book every two months, you will need to have the first three books already written before you launch book one. You can then write the other three as you are releasing the first ones.

Do you know how the series will progress?

If you want to write and publish quickly, do you have a plan for the series? Perhaps you don't use outlines, but you might still want to have an idea of what each book will cover. If you're an outliner, you definitely want to plan the series far enough in advance so that you can finish the books. Word count per month isn't the only thing that will determine if you can produce books quickly enough.

Do you have enough money to pay for editing and covers at this rate?

You'll need to have funds available to pay for editing and book covers or have enough money coming in each month to keep up with it. Work this out in advance and avoid the stress of writing books that you can't publish. Book your covers and editor ahead of time.

What is your launch plan? When will you start to advertise?

If you want to make a big push of the first book, do you have a launch plan? You don't want to get within days of releasing the first book and only then realize you have no plan to follow.

Have you researched the strategies other people have used? Several sources are mentioned in this article, and you can look at free videos on YouTube. Make sure you're not reinventing the wheel and listen to the hard-won knowledge of those who have gone before you. Most importantly, plan a release strategy that will keep you motivated while you enjoy the process. ■

Elaine Bateman

FULL OF FANFARE

GETTING THE WORD OUT ABOUT YOUR BOOK

W e've all been there: exhausted, over-caffeinated, and anxious about our next launch, wondering how to not just attract attention about our new release but how to also turn that initial buzz into a ravenous fandom. Regardless of whether you are preparing a launch every year or every month, turning readers into true fans continues to be important, mystical as it may seem. Somewhat like a secret sauce recipe.

Rachel L. Schade, author of two YA Epic Fantasy series, seems to

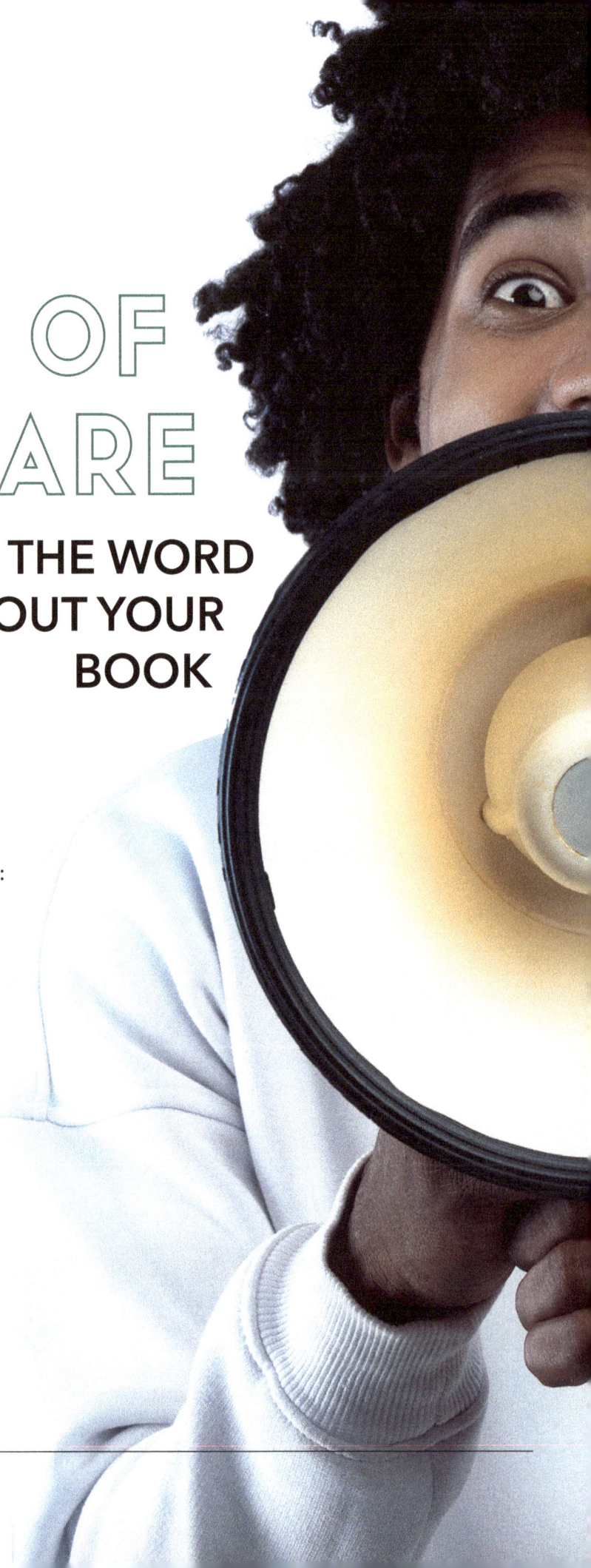

have figured out how to successfully conquer the mysticism. She offered a few practical ideas for how to approach your next launch with creativity, energy, and originality. Psst! Her new YA Epic Fantasy book, *Empire of Dragons*, garnered ten times as many pre-orders as any of her previous titles. So what did Rachel do differently this time?

GO WHERE THE READERS ARE

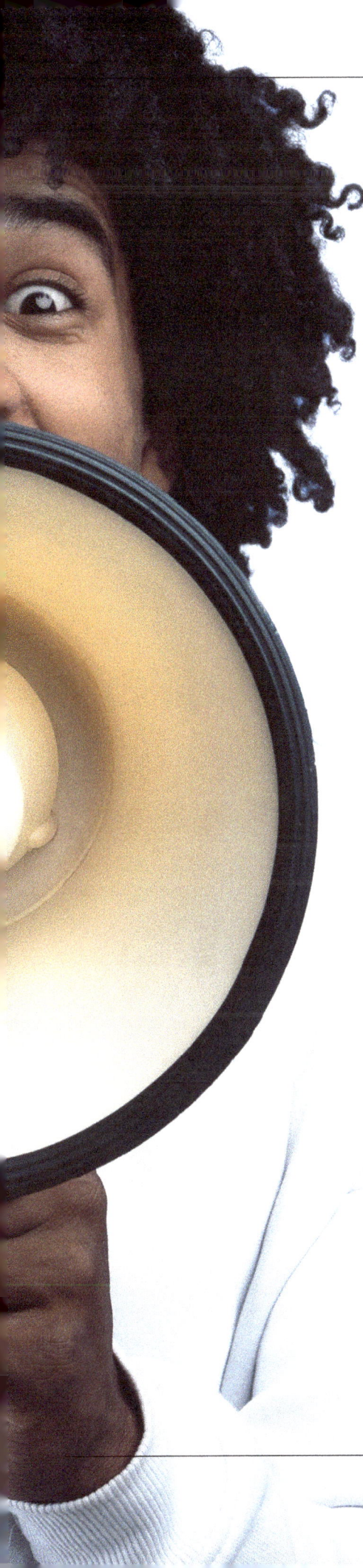

Creating hype on social media is not a novel idea, but authors raise concerns with the time commitment and effort involved as well as the uncertain pay-off. You can't and probably shouldn't even try to cover all channels. Instead, go where the readers in your niche hang out.

For example, Rachel decided to try some new-to-her media, including Instagram reels and TikTok videos, knowing that readers of YA Fantasy flock to those platforms. The effort she put into creating the social media content shines through. Rachel commissioned character art, an amazing bundle of covers, including a naked cover for her hardback, and pushed ahead with a reel featuring her cosplaying as the book's main character. Greek-goddess-style dress. Sparkling gold complexion. Hands all bloodied.

She also sought out niches of readers who vibe with the concepts and tropes in her books. If you scroll through the #dragonbooks on TikTok, you'll see plenty of her videos ranked near the top. But of course, this is not only applicable to YA Fantasy. Just ask all those spicy Romance authors how #spicytok is working out for them. And Facebook launch parties can still strike gold for various adult categories. Wink, wink, Reverse Harem.

GIVE FANS WHAT THEY ASK FOR

Once you have narrowed down the channels you will use to attract fans for your launch, you will need to brainstorm and create the right content. You can follow similar authors to see what they offer or interact with readers and filter through their suggestions.

This type of reader interaction drove Rachel out of her comfort zone and made her prioritize creating hardback editions of her books. Following specific reader requests, she even opened an Etsy shop to sell signed copies during the preorder period.

Sometimes the answers aren't so obvious, though, and you'll need to simply test what works. Rachel did this by creating a quote template and sharing a daily quote on her Instagram. She asked readers to share the posts to their stories, and they responded and interacted by trying to guess the character behind each quote.

"Posts, sharing quotes and excerpts, talking about your process, creating fun aesthetic videos—all of it makes the process fun and engaging for everyone. It makes potential readers curious about your books so they decide to check them out and join the fun."

KEEP IT FRESH AND FUN

Planning social media content for the launch can help you stock up on the right posts, reels, or videos, but leaving yourself some room for fun, new ideas could pay off as well. To get fresh insights, Rachel tapped into the suggestions of her street team. But how does one go about building a street team?

Consider where you should host your street team first. It should be your virtual corner, pleasant for you to use, and easy for the street team members to join. Ideally,

the environment should encourage discussions and spontaneous chats.

Rachel recruited her street team on Instagram, asking them to sign up via a Google form.

"My street team is separate from my ARC Team, as the only requirement is a willingness to help promote my books. I do try to engage with them regularly in a thread on Instagram to make the experience fun and personal and to offer them giveaways or e-ARCs."

The street team can create legitimacy and genuine hype at every step of the process from the first cover teaser to resharing raving reviews of your books. Visit Rachel's Instagram, and you'll find her stories filled with reposts of content shared by her street team. Shout-outs to the street team's posts make for varied content and can help you evade the dreaded salesy author trap.

"Definitely create a street team to help you spread the word organically. If you can find a few dedicated fans who are truly excited about your launch, their word of mouth can sell so many books for you without you having to spend a penny."

Once the team gets in the habit of sharing your book-related news, they seem to start doing that organically even before being asked to share. The frequent group chat interactions really come in handy here.

"If you can find a few dedicated fans who are truly excited about your launch, their word of mouth can sell so many books for you without you having to spend a penny."

Asking the street team about promo and content ideas makes members feel like an integral part of the process, which, in turn, increases their investment in the launch's success.

But above all else, Rachel highlights one major consideration for authors—having fun with the promo and launch activities.

"Most importantly, I'm having fun with it. I think when others see I genuinely am excited about these books and have fun talking about them, it makes them want to know more about what I write!"

The genuine hype created with all those interactions and activities allows Rachel to stick to the higher pricing she feels her lengthy Epic Fantasy books deserve. She credits her solid preorder marketing campaign for selling more books at $5.99 than she previously did at $2.99.

By now, you're probably sold on the importance of a dedicated street team and wondering how to find the time to run and maintain it. Rachel solved this exact conundrum by outsourcing the distribution of ARCs to a few different Instagram review tours, a Facebook group, and a paid service that sends ARCs to reviewers.

She also had a strategy in place to weed out non-participants from the street team. She asked members to sign up anew for her next book and hosted the new street team in a separate chat, adding additional members who expressed an interest. For

the third book in the series, she plans to repeat the process again to always keep the team engaged and excited about her books.

The tactics and ideas described here are in no way compulsory or exhaustive, although they've hopefully sparked your enthusiasm for everything that is possible for your next launch. Boldly follow your marketing senses and, as Rachel says, have fun with it! ■

Emilia Zeeland

Rocket Fuel Doesn't Come in a Can

WHY WIDE AUTHORS NEED A CUSTOM LAUNCH PLAN

"[O]ne of our tips is to think long-term and never to be obsessed, actually, about the launch. The launch is a very traditional publishing thing, when the books go into a physical bookstore and then they leave again."–Joanna Penn, Creative Penn podcast, Episode #575 (Sept 27, 2021) https://www.thecreativepenn.com/2021/09/27/co-writing-the-relaxed-author/

Book launch plans are all over the internet, including the twelve in my "Read Later" folder. They are fun to look at but can be dangerous for your author business.

You want your book to blast off into a fuel-efficient orbit and find more readers with every circuit. Why shouldn't you use a shiny launch plan?

How can you boost your new release without burning up all your resources? Build a control panel with these basic instruments to guide your mission through takeoff to orbit.

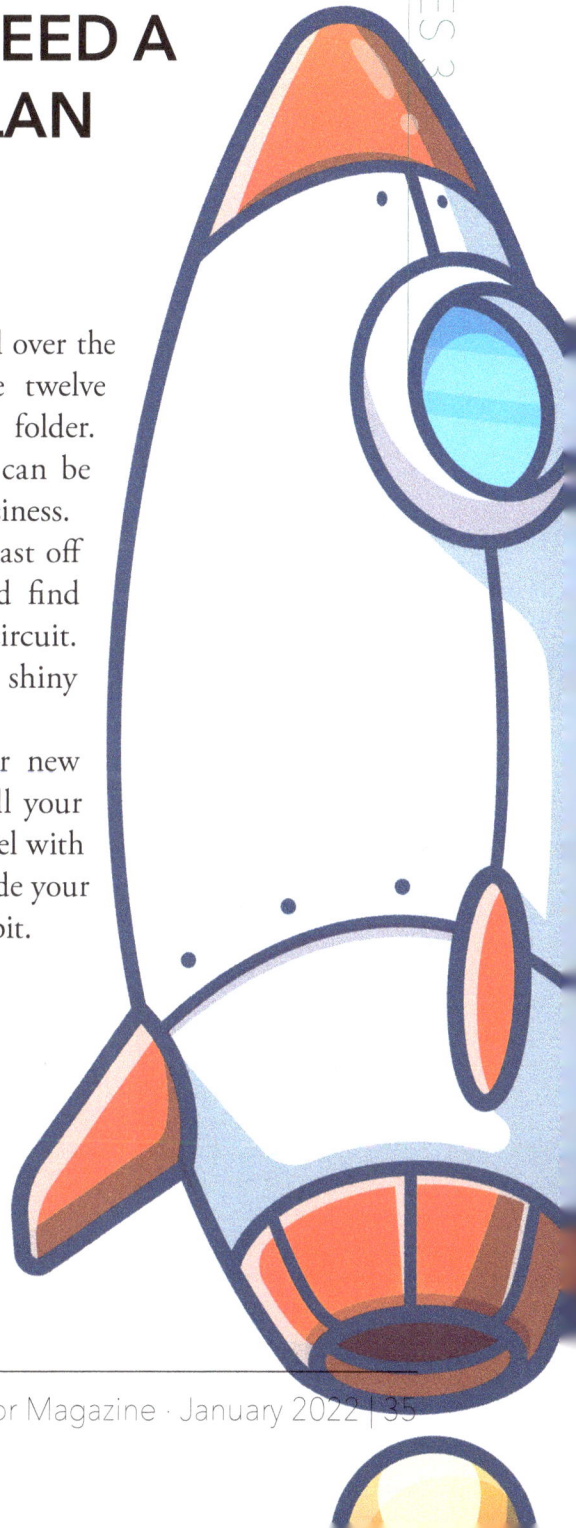

1. INVENTORY–ASSESS YOUR SITUATION

Use your creativity to come up with all the exciting ideas. If this isn't your first book, look back at your notes from earlier promotions and launches. Write about what you want this time and why. Here are some questions to start you off:

- What's your specific goal for this launch? Rank? Sales? Reviews? Subscribers?
- What have you already created that you could use?
- What worked last time?
- What do you want to test? What opportunities are you eyeing?
- What time and energy do you want to spend on launch activities?
- How can you connect this launch to previous and later releases?

Browse published launch plans for ideas, but sketch out your dream launch in all its messy glory.

2. INGREDIENTS–MAKE A ONE-SHEET

Uploading your book to wide retailers means repetitive detail work. Create a one-sheet with everything you need in one unformatted text file. From here, you can paste into many websites so that you don't have to deal with any bizarre formatting errors. After you're finished uploading, use the collected information to create a new page on your website and a downloadable one-sheet about your book. Include the following:

- Title, series name, and number
- Publication date
- ISBNs /ASINs for each format, LCCN if applicable
- One-sentence tagline
- Short description
- Trim size, shipping weight, permalink to book page on your website
- Categories, BISAC codes, Thema subjects, keywords, reading levels, age groups
- Reviews
- Prices

Build a control panel with these basic instruments to guide your mission through takeoff to orbit.

"Don't get too tied into the launch."–Joe Solari, 20Books Vegas 2021 Day 3 "The Myths of Money" 36:36 https://www.youtube.com/watch?v=n90g6ltM8_A

3. DECISIONS—SET YOUR BOOK UP FOR SUCCESS

Having one place to record your decisions can save you time, pain, and money. Make it quick and easy to access because you will refer to it again and again. The more decisions you make and the earlier you make them, the easier it is for other people to help you.

ISBN and formats: Decide—before you click submit—whether you will use your own consistent ISBNs for all your books or live with an awkward mishmash of free ISBNs from distributors. Once a book is on preorder, you can't change the ISBN or the title.

Price: Retail prices in all currencies take time and will require research. Many countries have laws requiring your books to be the same price across retailers. Retailers also require consistent pricing. Make your life easier with a table of prices by country: Retail, 40 percent off, and 99 cents. For example:

	A	B	C	D	F
1	Country	Currency	Full Price	40% off	0.99
2	Argentina	ARS	299	179.40	74.99
3	Australia	AUD	$7.99	$4.79	1.99
4	Bolivia	BOB	10	6.00	5
5	Brazil	BRL	9	5.40	4.99
6	Bulgaria	BGN	8.99	5.39	1.99
7	Canada	CAD	$4.99	$2.99	0.99
8	Chile	CLP	1300	780.00	600

Will you release at full price? Will you discount for one weekend for your newsletter subscribers? Will the new release be full price, and will the first in series be free or discounted?

Pro Tip: Schedule discounts after you've picked out your retailer promotions. Kobo's scheduling tool won't let you apply for a promotion if your book is already discounted. Apply first, then schedule discounts around that to match the rest of your plan.

Pro Tip: Leave time for price-matching if you plan to offer a wide book free on Amazon.

Publication date: The sooner you commit to a date, the sooner you can take advantage of opportunities. Your book may have a natural publication date because of a connection to a holiday or historical event or time of year. If not, choose one as soon as your book is past the last sticking point in the production process. I choose mine when the manuscript comes back from the developmental editor.

Preorder: Decide if you want to set up a preorder and when it will begin. Apple Books, Barnes & Noble, GooglePlay, and Kobo allow (and reward) preorders up to a year before the publication date. You'll need the title, ISBN, the actual or a placeholder cover, a brief description of the book, and categories. You can add and improve as publication approaches, but do yourself a favor and keep a consistent copy of the updated details in your one-sheet. You can customize these for each retailer. But don't make mistakes. Add your final upload deadline to your launch calendar.

Pro Tip: Goodreads will let you replace a placeholder book cover if it's obviously a placeholder.

Pro Tip: Kobo displays 5 percent of the manuscript as a preview. If you upload three chapters, as they suggest, then the store shows 5 percent of that. That's why they recommend you upload the finished file. If you use a placeholder file on any retailer, always include a note to the reader to contact you if they received the placeholder file instead of the final file by mistake.

Pro Tip: If you distribute through Draft2Digital (D2D) to Apple Books, D2D can turn off the preview setting for you. D2D recommends no placeholder files.

Promotion: Keep track of promotions you have applied for; paid newsletters or ads you have booked; and all other deadlines for awards, shared author promotions, planned giveaways, interviews, or editorial reviews you've decided to go for. If your book is accepted into a promotion, online bookstores don't always acknowledge it. Spread out your promotions to evaluate their effectiveness so your next launch will be even better.

December 1, 2021	Promo	Results
2		
3	Freebooksy newsletter for BOOK 1	A gazillion downloads
4		
5	Launch date for BOOK 3	Apple Books: 20 Kobo: 10 GooglePlay: 4

Protip: A simple grid with three columns will let you see dates, promotions as you plan them, and results. Use paper, whiteboard, Excel, or a word processor, whatever suits you. Colored pencils and stickers work well too. During a short promotion of a few days, you might plan something every day. A longer promotion can have gaps. Don't put yourself under pointless pressure.

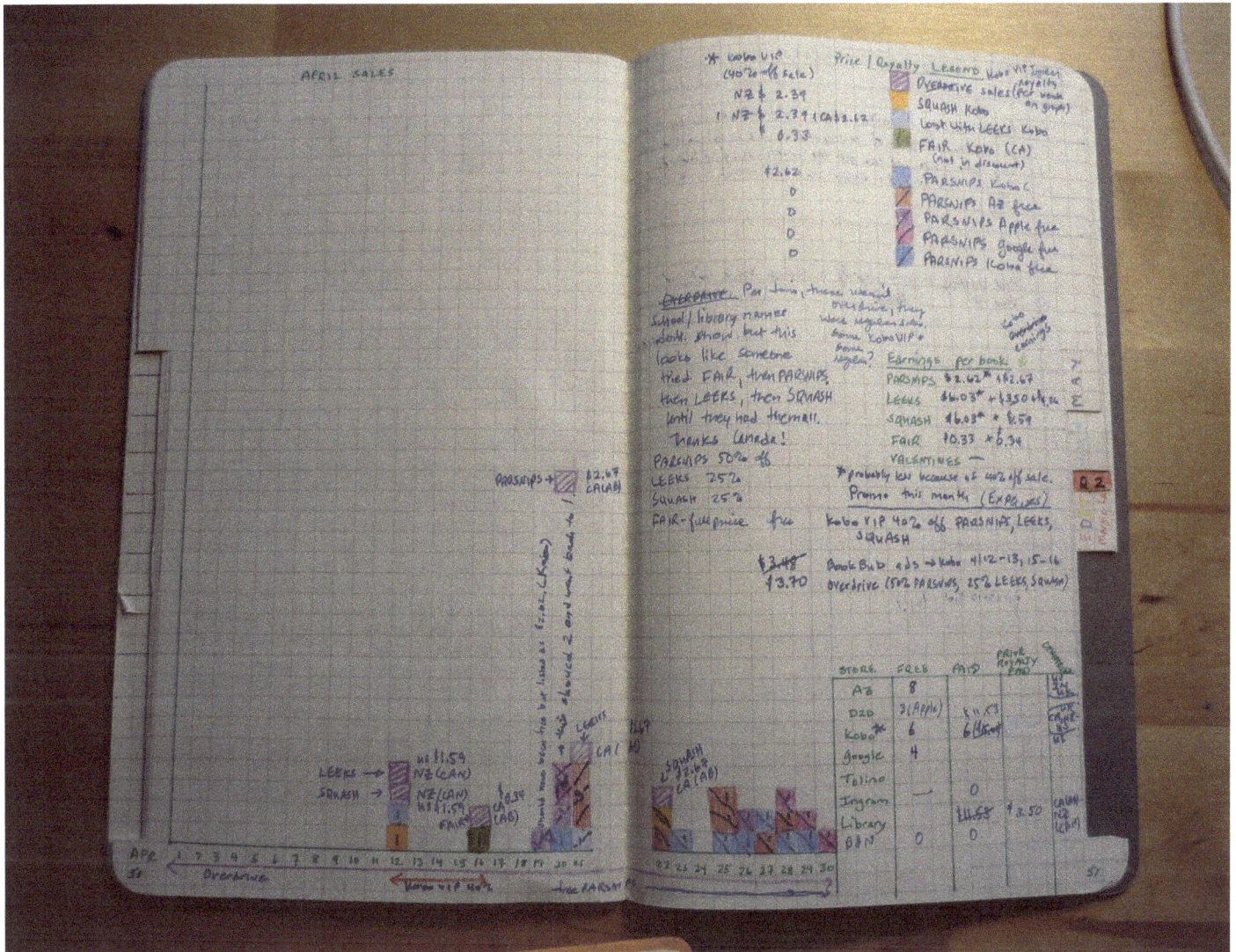

Pro Tip: Track results across multiple retailers. A tool like ScribeCount can keep track of many retailers, but IngramSpark sales aren't yet included. A graph is a quick way to plot downloads and sales as the launch progresses. Create a legend for downloads and sales by retailer with colored pencils. You can conveniently mark scheduled retailer promos under the date axis. Highlight important points to include in your next launch plan.

Partnerships: Consider group author promotions, newsletter swaps, email newsletter promotions, or promotions offered by organizations where you are a member or where your target audience is likely to be. Write down deadlines for sharing on your launch calendar.

4. CAPTURE AND CONNECT

Every time you send a new book out into the world, an engine fires in your publishing rocket. Use the momentum to strengthen the tie between your book and the reader. Here's a launch-by-launch example of how you could get more rocket fuel for your books over time:

Launch 1: A sign-up form for an email newsletter list with the link connecting the book to the newsletter in the backmatter of the book. This means you will be sending out a newsletter regularly, so you will have to think about what promise you are making to subscribers. Keep it simple.

Launch 2: A reader magnet that can be a reward or an incentive for the reader to sign up for your email newsletter

Launch 3: A preorder for the next book or short story in the same series or world with the link connecting your book to the book of the future.

Launch 4: An automation sequence that introduces the enticing qualities of your first book to your email newsletter setup. Persuade downloaders to become readers so they will want to read the rest of your books.

Launch 5: A permanently free or permanently 99 cent book can power up your publishing engines while you sleep.

Build in stages as you launch each book so that your rocket builds up enough momentum to break through the atmosphere, refuel at your international space station, and go into orbit.

5. LESSONS LEARNED—MAKE/UPDATE YOUR CHECKLIST

Here's where you try to understand what happened before the experience fades. Every launch requires a lot of effort under the pressure of time. Make this one count. Use your hard-won knowledge to refuel the rocket. Mark your calendar to check for a longer-term effect in the next weeks or months. Update your launch plan for the next book as a new release checklist.

"When you do that first launch and maybe it's just one more person that becomes a fan...[the base audience is] a little bigger, and that means the next launch is going to be a little bit better."—Joe Solari, 20Books Vegas 2021 Day 3 "The Myths of Money" 19:29. https://www.youtube.com/watch?v=n90g6ltM8_A ■

Laurel Decher

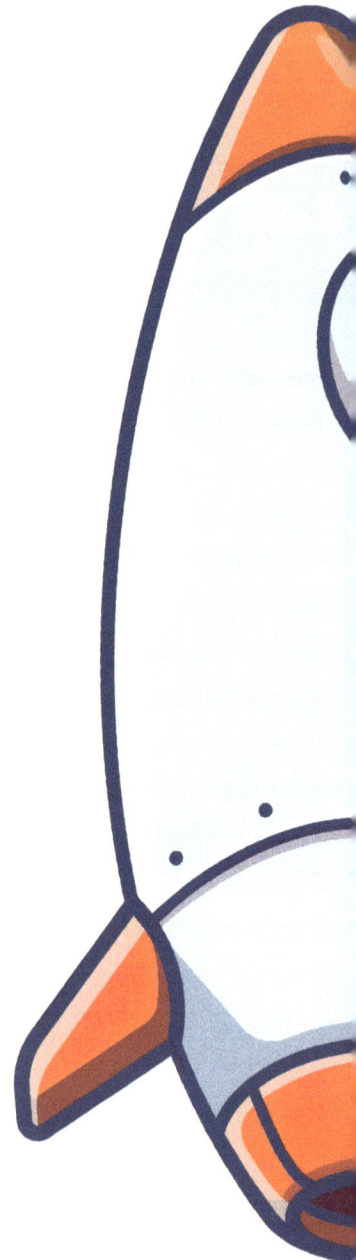

RESOURCES

"Plan Your Launch / Launch Your Plan." Alex Lidell. 20BooksVegas 2021 Day 3. https://www.youtube.com/watch?v=B54JN-PUBMTE&list=PLCl3DWM-P5iOtytsCGsdrLmfjqQjAH-8Jm&index=98

Publishing IndieRoute 101—from Alice Briggs.

BookBub. The Ultimate Guide to Promoting a Book Launch (email sign-up required) https://insights.bookbub.com/book-launch-checklist-marketing-timeline-traditionally-published-authors

About Preorders

GooglePlay Preorders: https://support.google.com/books/partner/answer/2364635?hl=en

Kobo Preorders: https://kobowritinglife.zendesk.com/hc/en-us/articles/360059386491-KWL-Guide-to-Pre-Orders

Amazon Preorders: https://kdp.amazon.com/en_US/help/topic/G201499380

Apple Books Preorders: https://itunespartner.apple.com/books/articles/set-up-a-book-pre-order-2733 (Note: These are the directions for authors direct with Apple Books. You can do many of the same things via a distributor.)

Draft2Digital Preorders (distributor): https://www.draft2digital.com/faq

Print Preorders with IngramSpark: https://www.ingramspark.com/blog/on-sale-date-for-book-marketing

Tracking Tools

ScribeCount https://www.scribecount.com/

Wide Wizard https://widewizard.co/

THE COMMOTION OF NOTION

ORGANIZING THE WORKFLOWS OF WRITING

Notion is the organizing tool I didn't know I needed but now can't live without. The slick web and mobile app interfaces collect notes, tasks, and projects together into a single Swiss Army knife of information. Other tools might do a few things better, but I've found nothing else that does so much so easily.

What makes Notion so easy is its drag-and-drop interface, which allows users to create blocks of content and move them around and across any number of pages. These blocks include paragraphs, headers, to-do lists, URLs, images, embedded files, and more that can be built into a staggering variety of interlinked pages.

Many of the adaptable templates conform to most any writer's unique workflow. I keep finding new uses for Notion and still haven't scratched the surface.

Here are a few things I've used Notion for:

A TIME-TRACKER

Notion's project management features can be used to assign tasks and track the time spent performing them. I can tell at a glance whether I've been productive with my time and where I need to shift my efforts.

For freelance projects, I've set up a column of blocks for each day of the week and have a reference I can use to prepare my invoices. I can drag blocks around the time-tracker as my priorities change and alter the existing blocks as new projects arise.

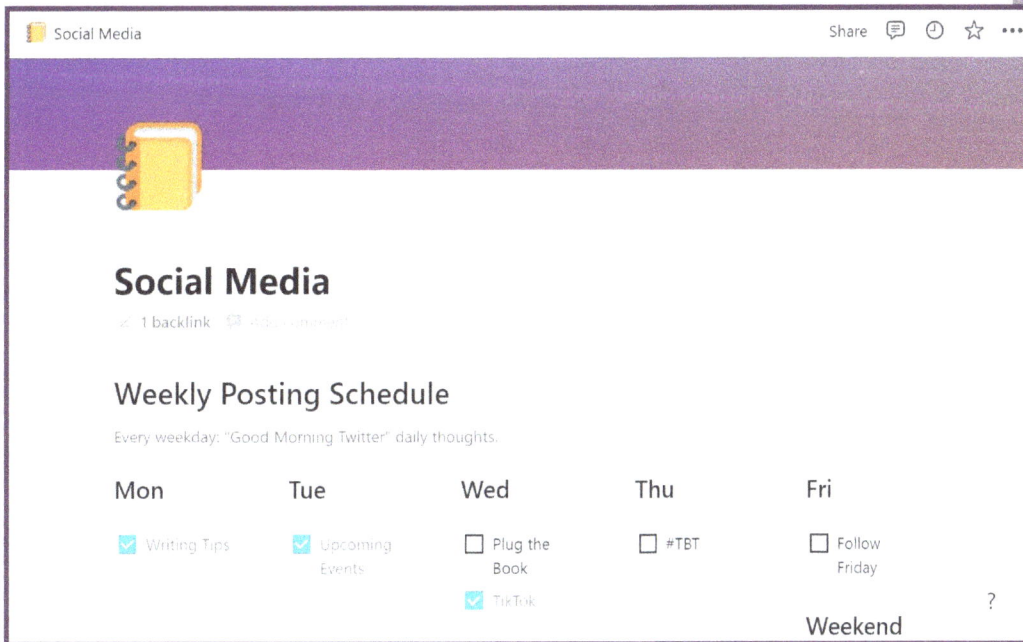

Social Media

1 backlink

Weekly Posting Schedule

Every weekday: "Good Morning Twitter" daily thoughts.

Mon	Tue	Wed	Thu	Fri
☑ Writing Tips	☑ Upcoming Events	☐ Plug the Book	☐ #TBT	☐ Follow Friday
		☑ TikTok		

?

Weekend

A TO-DO LIST

I've set up my to-do list as a database. Several views are available, including a grid with columns that I've arranged by urgency from ASAP to Maybe Someday. Each task can be set with a due date, and Notion will send me reminders as the deadlines approach.

A typical task in my ASAP column is titled "Write an Article About Notion." Clicking the block opens a sub-page that includes the assignment sheet from my editor, some initial notes I've made, links to information I need to complete the task, and an embedded Google Docs file where I'm typing these words right now.

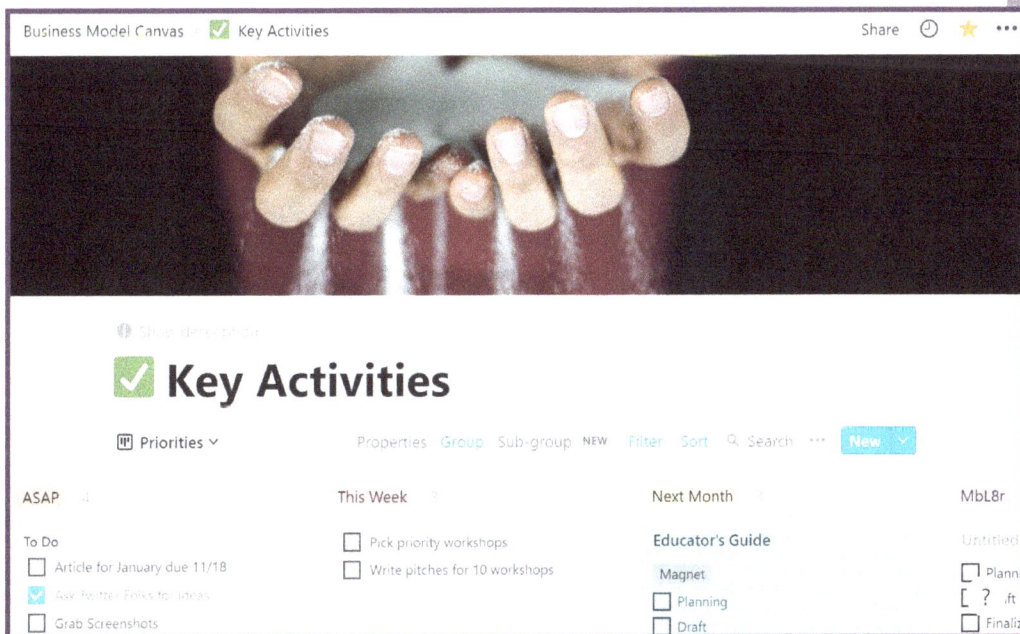

Business Model Canvas / ☑ Key Activities

☑ Key Activities

▥ Priorities ⌄   Properties Group Sub-group NEW Filter Sort 🔍 Search ⋯ **New** ⌄

ASAP	This Week	Next Month	MbL8r
To Do		Educator's Guide	Untitled
☐ Article for January due 11/18	☐ Pick priority workshops	Magnet	☐ Planni
☑ Ask Twitter Folks for ideas	☐ Write pitches for 10 workshops	☐ Planning	[?].ft
☐ Grab Screenshots		☐ Draft	☐ Finali

A COOL CATCHER

I found something cool on the internet today, which happens all the time. I like to collect these for future reference. I used to keep dozens of open browser tabs, but now I can use Notion's Chrome extension to place the bookmarks into my links database with a Ctrl-Shift-K. Notion then allows me to add a note to each link, reminding me why I originally thought it was important, sort it into a category with similar links, and tag it with whatever projects it might best apply to.

Things can migrate from my cool catcher into my to-do list, project notes, reading list, or any other place they're needed.

AN EXPENSE TRACKER

I use Notion to keep a handy list of writing-related expenses, copies of invoices, and monthly budget in one place that's quick to update. When the pile of blocks is too much to handle, I can embed an Excel or Google Sheets version to hand off to my accountant during tax season.

A BUSINESS PLANNER

Many people I know maintain a business plan for their writing. I use a format called the business model canvas, which creates a one-page visual dashboard. The interactive version I made on Notion uses toggle lists to keep additional details in a more compact form and links to subpages for a deeper dive into costs, revenue, stakeholders, services, reader outreach, and other areas.

As a side note, I use color coding and lots of emojis for visual appeal. Every page on Notion can have its own distinct header design and an icon that appears in the menus and tabs. The design is flexible but always looks clean and user-friendly, including the optional dark mode.

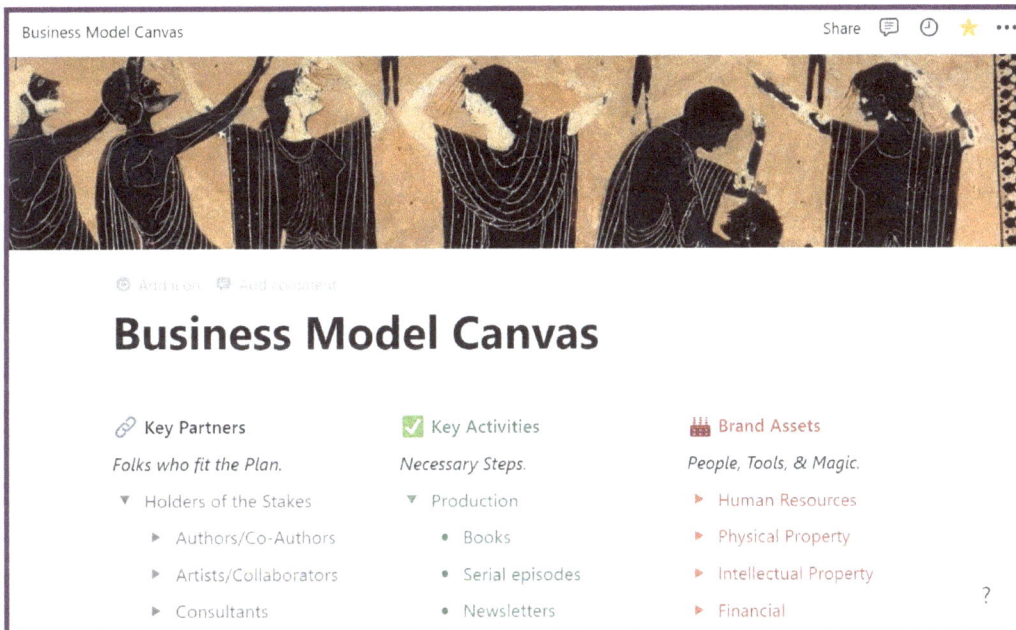

A PLAYLIST WRANGLER

I like to make book soundtracks with different types of music and different moods to play while I'm writing different types of scenes. Although these lists and songs may exist in a number of different places, Notion works well with multimedia content and can help sort and collect a variety of links and embeds into a single place.

A RESOURCE DIRECTORY

Artists and authors are advised to view themselves as brands and to present an intentional and consistent image. For the sake of version control and consistency, I maintain a branding directory in Notion that includes current and historical versions of my biography in a variety of lengths, a headshot, book and series descriptions, cover art, links, etc.

When I need a specific image or a bit of text, I can quickly and easily grab it. And when I need to update any of these elements of branding, it helps that each one has a list of all the websites and social media profiles where it exists out in the public-facing world.

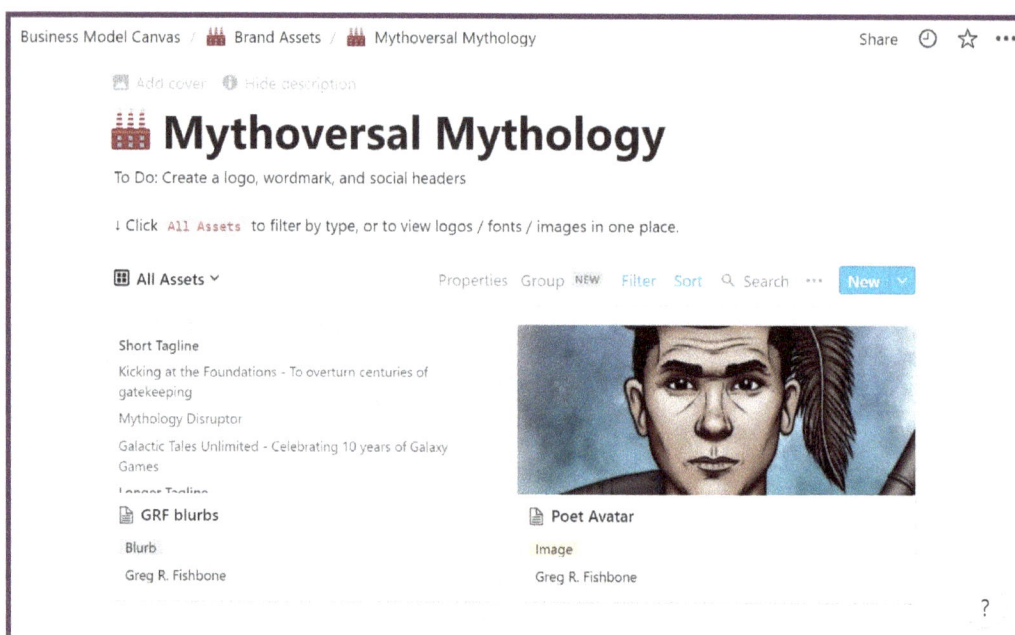

A SOCIAL MEDIA PLANNER

I keep a list of my most commonly used hashtags on a Notion page, divided by book and social media platform. This makes the tags available and editable from either my laptop or phone and ready to paste into any social media post. I could do the same for content templates. Since individual tweets can be stored as Notion blocks, I also maintain a Social Media Hall of Fame and Shame for reference.

For quick access, I've marked my social media pages as favorites, which puts them into a separate menu. A widget on my iPhone also lists these favorited pages, making them accessible from my phone's home screen with a single push of a button.

Hashtags

Last week's character of the week was Pyrrha, one of the main characters from the upcoming BECOMING HERCULES Vella serial by G. Fishbone. Pyrrha's original story in Greek mythology is lost to us, except for the evidence of her hero cult in the city of Thebes.
https://mythoversal.com/w/mythic/a/pyrrha-character

#greekmyth #greekmyths #greekmythology #disrupttexts #becominghercules #hercules #heracles #mythology #myth #pjo #vella #kindlevella #mg #middlegrade #ya #youngadult #mgfantasy #yafantasy #fantasy #readercommunity

GETTING A NOTION

You can snag a free Personal Plan account at http://notion.so and gain access to all the features described in this article. Although it's called "personal," the plan will allow you to invite up to five collaborators to share pages privately. You can also make pages available for public view.

A Personal Pro Plan grants individuals an unlimited number of private collaborators for four dollars a month or as a free upgrade for students and educators. Other benefits of the Personal Pro Plan include access to thirty days of version history and unlimited storage for uploaded files, versus 5Mb for the regular Personal Plan.

CAVEATS

Notion is a tool to organize your activities and workflow but not a vault for your most valued secrets. Without end-to-end encryption, third parties could possibly access your data. Therefore, I'd advise against using Notion to store passwords or banking information.

And what if the Notion servers ever go offline? To guard against the possible loss of your data, you'll want to create periodic backups using the export function for the HTML pages and subpages that Notion generates, while data in a Notion database can be saved in CSV format for upload into the spreadsheet of your choice.

One other caveat is that like most tech, Notion has a learning curve. The basics are easy enough to pick up, but you will want to explore many features in order to achieve the greatest possible benefit.

SUMMING UP

Notion is a free-to-use and cheap-to-upgrade organizational tool and knowledge repository with flexible web and mobile app interfaces. With a small investment of time and effort, the platform can be adapted to the unique needs of just about any author. If you use Notion, consider sharing your own solutions with the rest of the community. ∎

Greg Fishbone

MERCH FOR AUTHORS

Branded merch on Etsy, Amazon, and your own site.
Learn about extended stock licenses.
Includes sample contracts.

envato elements

Travel & Hotel Email Builder
By theemon

Travel Email Builder
By HyperPix

Kant - Email Template
By ThemeMountain

Olive - Fashion Email Template
By giantdesign

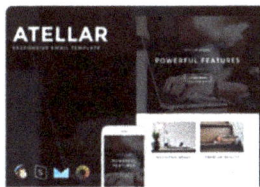

Metro App - Instapage Template
By Merad

ButaPest Email Template
By jeetuG

All the Email Templates you need and many other design elements, are available for a monthly subscription by subscribing to Envato Elements. The subscription costs $16.50 per month and gives you **unlimited access** to a massive and growing library of **1,500,000+** items that can be downloaded as often as you need (stock photos too)!

Tech Tools

Courtesy of IndieAuthorTools.com
Got a tool you love and want to share with us?
Submit a tool at IndieAuthorTools.com

T2M URL SHORTENER
T2M is an affordable all-in-one platform for URL shortening & branded links management.
https://t2mio.com/

TICKTICK
Join millions of people to capture ideas, organize life, and do something creative everyday.
https://ticktick.com/

KRISP
Sound Clear in Online Meetings
AI-powered app that removes background noise and echo from meetings leaving only human voice.
https://krisp.ai/

FREEDOM
Freedom to be incredibly productive.
Freedom is the app and website blocker for Mac, Windows, Android, iOS, and Chrome, used by over 2,000,000 people to reclaim focus and productivity.
https://freedom.to/

FIREALPACA
FireAlpaca is the free Digital Painting Software that is compatible with both Mac and Windows.
https://firealpaca.com

Walking the Wire

ADDING TENSION TO YOUR STORIES

Tension is not just reserved for Thrillers—it spans across all genres. In Romance, there's sexual tension (just kiss already!); in Dystopia, there's the ever-present threat that one wrong move could draw the attention of the government; in Horror, we have things that go bump in the night (which may or may not cause bodily harm to our characters).

But it doesn't end there.

In *How to Write a Page Turner*, Jordan Rosenfeld says that the four key building blocks of tension are danger, conflict, uncertainty, and withholding. Where there's danger, there's tension. Where there's conflict between characters, there's tension. Where the outcome is uncertain, there's tension. And where there are secrets, there's tension.

Below, we explore the different ways authors can infuse their stories with tension.

CONFLICT

According to K.M. Weiland, tension is the threat of conflict. It's the anticipation of conflict that keeps readers on the edge of their seats. But tension can also drive conflict.

Broadly speaking, conflict stems from the forces that prevent the protagonist from achieving their goals, from the obstacles they must overcome on their journey. These obstacles could take the form of other characters (not just classic evil antago-

> Conflict stems from the forces that prevent the protagonist from achieving their goals, from the obstacles they must overcome on their journey.

nists—these could include love interests in Romance), or they could be broader, like man vs. nature (especially in the Post-Apocalyptic genre), or man vs. society (Dystopia).

Because conflict takes many forms, authors have a multitude of options for injecting conflict—and therefore tension—into their stories.

IMMINENT DANGER

According to Rosenfeld, danger includes threats to the physical, emotional, or psychological well-being of the character. When the character is in danger, our fight-or-flight instincts kick in. If a reader is invested in a character, they want to make sure they get out alive—and they won't stop reading till they know for sure. When done well, the reader will be glued to their book, turning pages just to see whether the character managed to thwart the danger and escape to safety.

GIVING READERS INFORMATION

Provide the reader with information relevant to the story on a need-to-know basis. This is similar to Rosenfeld's concept of withholding information. While reading, the reader is asking questions. Knowing when to answer them can greatly enhance the story. As authors, we don't want to string readers along forever without giving them anything in return. Doing so could result in the readers putting your book down—and not picking it up again.

For example, the Reaping in *Hunger Games* is not explained until Katniss (and the reader) experiences it. Although it is mentioned multiple times, the author never gives us a definition. She knows the readers are wondering what it is, and she satisfies their curiosity at just the right movement. This technique keeps readers turning the pages—they have an urge to find the answer. And when they do, it's all the more satisfying. Presenting readers with information when they need to know it and not info-dumping is a sign of trusting the intelligence of the reader.

Let's say your heroine has a secret. She knows what it is, you (the author) know what it is, but the reader doesn't. The heroine purposefully doesn't reveal it early on. The readers will feel compelled to keep turning the pages to find out her secret (which can double as her motivation). In this scenario, it'll be most effective when revealed in a conversation.

Similarly, the heroine may want to find and kill someone, but she doesn't say why. Is it because she's a bounty hunter and it's her job?

Is it because this person killed her parents? Or maybe this person was an old friend or flame who betrayed her. The reader can speculate, but the only way they can know for sure is to keep turning the pages.

ANTICIPATION

Tease readers with what's coming–but don't give them the answer immediately. K.M. Weiland says to draw it out as much as possible but not so much that they either get bored or stop caring about what awaits the characters at the end. Drop little hints for your readers here and there—close some loops while opening new ones. That way, you will drag readers through the story.

MINI CLIFFHANGERS

Mini cliffhangers at the end of chapters can be a great tool to keep readers on their toes. They can be as simple as a telephone ringing in an otherwise empty house, hearing a twig snap in the backyard, or seeing the love interest with another woman.

Mini cliffhangers are especially effective when writing dual or multiple points of view (POV). Start a new POV right after the mini cliffhanger—readers won't have a choice but to whizz past the next POV to find out what happens. As a bonus, end all your chapters on mini cliffhangers to keep readers turning the pages and reading till the early hours, muttering to themselves, "Just one more chapter." They will keep coming back for more, and your stories will be truly unputdownable.

AUTHOR BEWARE

Tension is just as much about employing certain techniques as knowing what to avoid. Below, we list several points that authors should avoid if they want to create tension-filled stories.

MAKING THINGS "TOO EASY"

Conflict and threats that are too easily resolved for the characters drain tension from our stories. The same can be said for danger that is too far away or not imminent enough. If there is no real threat to the characters, why should they care? And, by extension, why should the readers care? Make sure that the threats your character faces are real and difficult to overcome. Then readers will sense the tension seeping from your pages.

INFO DUMPS

Info-dumping is giving away large chunks of information all at once. In fiction, these could range from world-building to backstory (providing details from the protagonist's childhood that have no relevance or bearing on the plot). In Fantasy and Sci-Fi, examples could include providing the history or origin of fantastical or alien races. Info dumps can give away information that would be more effective when revealed piece by piece later in the story.

While you may be fascinated by and want your readers to know the trade routes of wool in your epic fantasy, exercise caution—minute details like this probably don't belong in your novel unless, of course, they are crucial to the plot.

MUNDANE ACTIONS

Using quotidian actions, such as brushing teeth or going for a grocery run, can dramatically slow down the pace and kill the tension in your story. Even sitting around a table or campfire (common in Fantasy) and eating dinner can get repetitive. Used these scenes sparingly, in particular as a backdrop to an important conversation that drives the plot forward. We read to escape the mundane, to see the world through the eyes of someone with an exciting life. We don't need to read about the same tasks that we perform every day in our fiction.

CONCLUSION

Tension can take many shapes and forms. Whether it's through infusing conflict or danger, providing readers with information when they need to know it, using techniques such as mini cliffhangers, or avoiding the mundane and ordinary, there's a tension technique for everyone. So go forth, and make your stories tense and unputdownable! ■

Kasia Lasinska

Don't DIY Your Website...

CIY Your Website

Cohort (noun) /ˈkōˌhôrt/ - A group of people banded togheter as a group.

Build your WordPress website in 4 weeks with a group of other authors, led by a WordPress expert. Create a gorgeous functional site from scratch without spending thousands on a designer.

HTTPS://WRITELINK.TO/IATU

Podcasts We Love

Author Revolution

This podcast that promises to help you get clear on how to move forward, as well as hand over actionable tips on what you can do to get your novel published as quickly as possible, without sacrificing quality.

https://authorrevolution.org/

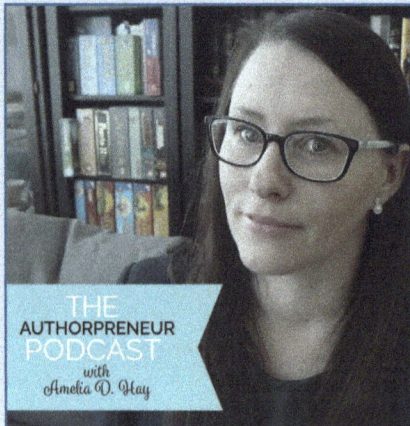

The Authorpreneur Podcast

Writing, Self-Publishing, and Book Marketing Advice for Writers

https://authorpreneurpodcast.com/podcast/

Book Launch Show

Follow along as book launch expert Tim Grahl teaches you the fundamentals of launching a bestselling book. Based on his work with hundreds of authors and launching dozens of top New York Times, Wall Street Journal, and other bestselling books, he will share the insights and step-by-step tactics you can use to launch your own successful book.

https://booklaunchshow.simplecast.com/

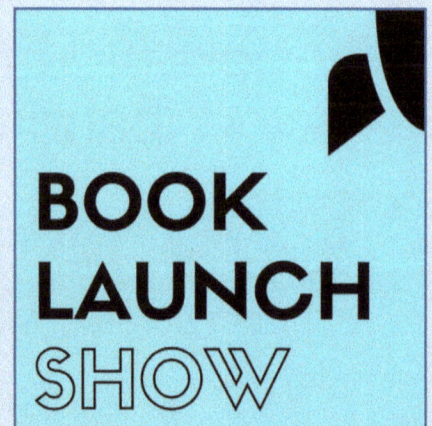

The Balance of Magic

USING FENG SHUI TO FRAME YOUR MAGIC SYSTEM

Magic systems can be one of the most fun parts of world building. Readers also obsess over this part of fantasy. They are looking for clearly laid-out rules, so many authors base their fantasies off known systems. This gives readers something familiar, allowing them to fill in any blanks that might exist.

Feng shui offers an excellent basis for your magic system. Feng shui is the Chinese practice of geomancy—that is, the location of where objects are placed is significant and affects the energy of surroundings. This is true both for where objects are set down physically and where they are located in time and space. This ideology has been in practice for thousands of years and can be divided into two schools of thought: The Form school, which focuses on what can be seen with the naked eye, and The Compass school, which focuses on qi—or chi, the life-force energy that we cannot see. If you want to delve a little deeper into these practices, we recommend checking out Feng Shui Nexus for a great, simplified overview.

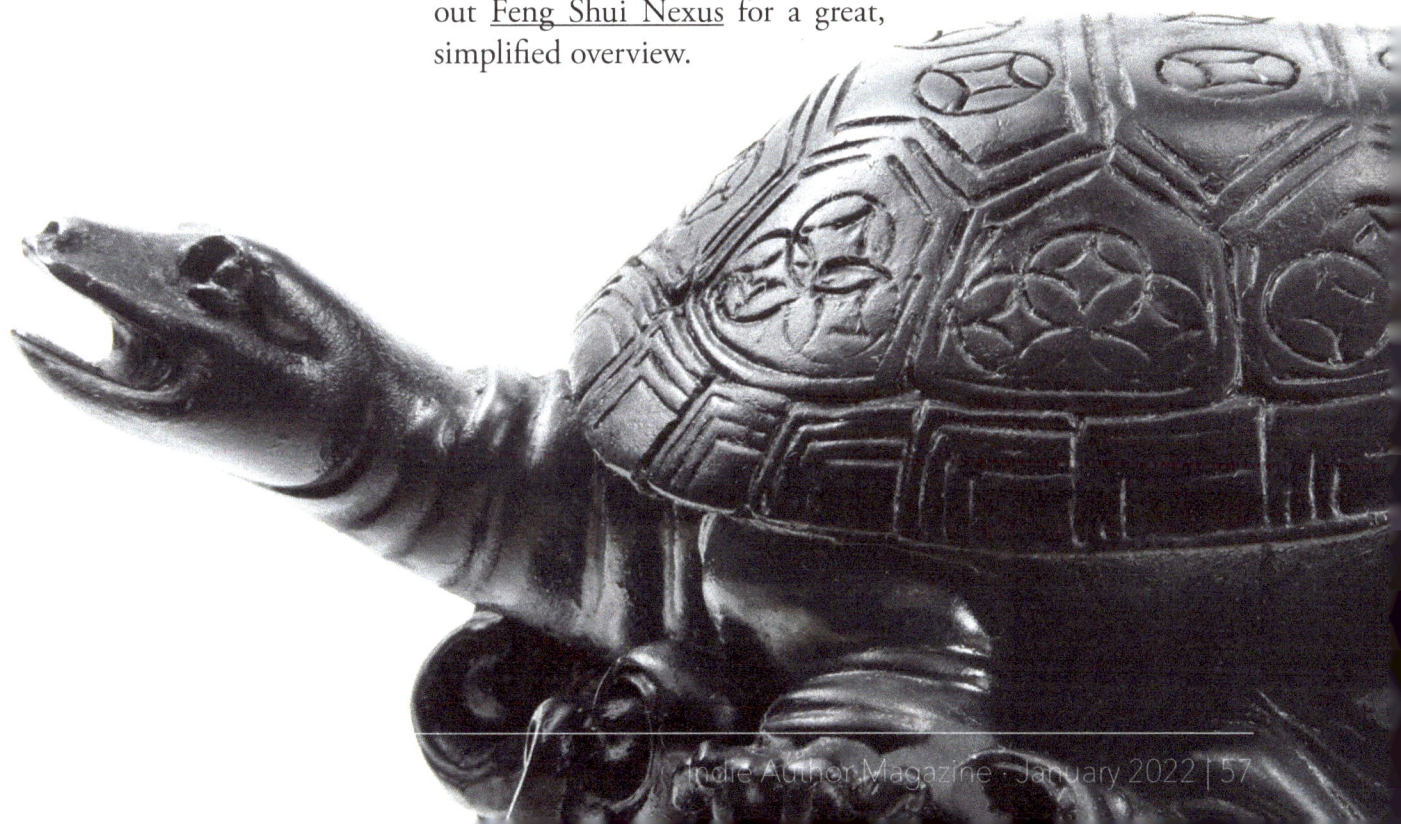

Feng Shui literally means "wind-water" and thus is heavily guided by the elements. The official Five Elements—water, wood, fire, earth, and metal—are the most significant. They exist in a natural cycle: water to grow wood, wood to spark fire, fire to create earth, earth to create metal, and metal to attract water (i.e., condensation). These elements make up all of creation and are considered dominant, depending on the material makeup of objects and beings.

For our purposes in developing a magic system for our made-up worlds, we need to focus on how the energy of these elements affects each other positively and negatively. They can simply exhaust each other or destroy each other, depending on the element in question. These inter-connections are logical conclusions. For example, if there is too much of one type of energy over another, they might cause an imbalance or bad luck for our protagonists. For example, too much water puts out fire. Medicines and rituals fall under these elemental guidelines that our protagonist and support characters might want to consider in their quests.

Polarity, which results from the yin-yang theory, is another important aspect. We could apply this principle to our antagonists to make them the perfect counter to our heroes. Our antagonist's strengths are our hero's weaknesses. Often we see this in our hero having a big heart and the antagonist appearing cold-hearted.

Astrology is a huge factor in a person's qi as it determines the dominant energy forces in their life, revealing their strengths and weaknesses. This can help us shape the conflicts our protagonists will face and how they'll solve them. For instance, 1986 is the Tiger year, and the element assigned to that cycle was fire, so someone born that year is a Fire Tiger. Astrology can also be used to make calendars for our worlds, determining their seasons. We can play with this on a cosmic scale and decide whether the planet we set our story in is Earth-like or more alien. Adjusting the number of visible celestial bodies in the sky, such as constellations, moons, and other planets, could have all kinds of interesting implications in our worlds and their energies.

Tools to consider for determining and measuring qi over the centuries have been calendars, rulers, astrolabes, and magnetic compasses. Most importantly, sacred texts are key to guiding practitioners. These objects give authors plenty of fuel to create gizmos and gadgets that add color and depth to story worlds. We can be as serious or facetious as we desire. Who wouldn't want to create the cult of the sacred protractor?

We've barely scratched the surface of feng shui. One could spend a lifetime researching all its tenets and complexities. It just goes to show that some of the oldest teachings still give us great fuel for thinking. ▪

Sine Mairi MacDougall

What Is Women's Fiction?

In a sentence, Women's Fiction is written by women for women. It isn't that the genre is exclusive; men can and have read Women's Fiction titles. However, the author writes with the female reader in mind. Relational sagas, love stories, and generational stories all make up the commercially written books that tap into the reader's desire to grow with characters through their sometimes-larger-than-life but mostly relatable problems.

THE DIFFERENCE BETWEEN WOMEN'S FICTION AND ROMANCE

There is a line—albeit very fine—between Women's Fiction and Romance. But it is there. In a Romance, the central relationship is between two characters. These characters will encounter conflict that brings them growth so that they are eventually together happily ever after.

Women's Fiction could be a story about two characters, but both of them come with a cast of characters that are on the growth arc with them. The characters could be siblings, friends, family, or a strong cast of coworkers.

The issues in Women's Fiction rise above the "does he like me, do I like him?" dance that is common in Romance. These characters deal

with issues like drug abuse, alcoholism, divorce, death of a loved one, caring for aging parents, and illnesses that disrupt life patterns.

Women's Fiction primarily follows the growth arc of the main female character. The other characters will have moments of maturity, but the reader is invested in the female lead rising above her problems and walking away from the situation as a new person, a better version of herself, and, regardless of the outcome, at peace with herself.

Women's Fiction focuses on life issues unlike the light-hearted feel of Chick-Lit.

WHY READ OR WRITE WOMEN'S FICTION?

Women's Fiction stories include a relatable protagonist: the lady next door, your mother's best friend, or your younger or older sister.

The men in these stories struggle as well. They are attractive in their own way—meaning they are pleasing to the main character's eye, but they may not be posing as a shirtless cover model.

Because of the large cast in Women's Fiction stories, the ages vary as their issues transcend arbitrary timelines. Divorce happens to people young and old. A sudden illness is disarming regardless of when it strikes. Characters grapple with the universal desires to belong to a community, fit in with family, and have that friend that understands them almost better than they understand themselves.

Our close-knit community of characters doesn't have all the answers. They want to do the right thing if only they knew exactly what it was and how to do it. Words from smart friends, coworkers, the potential love interest, and occasionally, the wise-beyond-their-years child guide the protagonist on her growth arc.

While immersed in a Women's Fiction novel, the reader is at the table drinking a cup of coffee with the characters—sometimes giving advice she may or may not follow. Other times, the exchange is the other way around, and the reader is delighted by the heartwarming outcome of what was originally a tough situation.

And this is why we enjoy reading and writing Women's Fiction stories. She makes the right decision for her.

COMMON TROPES IN WOMEN'S FICTION

Slice of life: The mundane moments in life are great for revealing the character's normal or what the character strives to have as status quo.

Family secret: There are two types of family secrets: "don't tell mom, dad, or grandma because it will disappoint them" and a secret with the potential to disrupt the lives of the people the main character loves. Scrambling, stress, and what-ifs

become the internal and external conflict for the protagonist.

Coming home: The character has been away from the community for years and has decided to return to their roots—and face the factors that convinced her that living anyplace else would be better. The story ends with her realization that she belongs in her childhood town.

Seasoned (or later-in-life) romance: The main character will find love. She may be widowed, divorced, a career woman, or with a lifestyle that offered no opportunity for her to embrace a romantic relationship. Now is her time to find that someone special.

Friendship: She has friends who know her flaws and love her in spite of them. The friends offer support and wisdom. Conflict provides a moment of growth for both of them.

Community: The protagonist is active in her community. If she doesn't attend the town council meeting, one of her friends does and reports the information back to her. She participates in all the events that make her town special.

Second-chance romance: If the character is divorced or in the midst of a struggling relationship, she will come back to pursue the love they once had. Alternatively, the main character had a chance at romance, but for some reason, it never happened. Life has been kind enough to grant them another chance at love. ◼

Merri Maywether

GETTING THE MOST FROM YOUR WRITING TIME

How many times have you heard yourself say, "If only I had more time to write"? Probably far too many. One popular and well-proven method of increasing your productivity within your available time is to alternate periods of focused work (also called "sprints") with short rest breaks.

THE POMODORO TECHNIQUE

The Pomodoro technique is a time management system developed by Francesco Cirillo in the late 1980s. While there are many phone apps available, you can easily use the timer on your phone or, as Cirillo did, use a kitchen timer—tomato-shaped or otherwise.

Cirillo's five steps follow:

1. Choose your task
2. Set a timer for twenty-five minutes
3. Work for twenty-five minutes
4. Take a five-minute break. Repeat.
5. Take a longer break after completing four Pomodoros.

Obviously, these steps are not prescriptive. If you have an hour available, you might want to do shorter Pomodoros, so divide the sixty minutes into two fifteen-minute writing periods, two five-min-

utes breaks, and wrap up with a twenty-minute writing sprint. It's all about discovering what works best for you.

MOTIVATION, GOALS, AND REWARDS

Sprints work very well when done in groups and are great for maintaining motivation and focus. They have the added benefit of accountability as, during the shorts breaks, you can catch up with the rest of the group and share your progress. Writing is an isolated activity, but this camaraderie makes it less so.

During sprint sessions, you can also give yourself small rewards for hitting self-imposed targets. These can be as simple as a cup of coffee, an episode of a favorite show, or a gold star on your calendar, but they can make a huge difference to your word count.

Why not give Pomodoros and/or Sprints a try? They can be quite productive, add variety to your daily writing, and offer a fun yet effective way to reach your writing goals. ■

Jac Harmon

ONE STEP AT A TIME

Indie authors have so much to think about and learn, and that's before you even tackle the world's most enormous to-do list. There's writing, editing, finding beta and ARC readers, social media, emailing your list, and on and on. Oh yes, and having a life!

So how do you get it all done without going completely bonkers or deciding that particle physics really would be a much easier career?

Well, you don't! If you think about that huge pile of tasks and try to accomplish them all, you will probably become overwhelmed, won't be able to decide where to even begin, or run off and join the circus.

Instead, try picking just a couple of things tonight that you have to do tomorrow. Not ten or twenty. Just two or three. Then pick the most urgent or important one and do that first. Focus only on that, on what's right in front of you, then move on the next task and the next until you're done.

If you still have time in your day, you can tackle something else, but you'll have finished the most important things first.

If you can focus on what's most important right now while still keeping in mind your long-term plans and goals, you'll have the perfect mix for staying productive.

Pro Tip: Outsource as much as you can that you really don't need to or want to do yourself. Take a look at our article on outsourcing from October's issue if you haven't already (https://indieauthormagazine.com/business-shifts-beat-burnout-and-grow-your-team-with-outsourcing/). Joanna Penn has a great book, *Productivity for Authors* (https://www.thecreativepenn.com/productivitybook/), that also talks about outsourcing, among other relevant topics.

As you go, you'll probably find faster and more effective ways of working that suit you. And if you need help, don't be afraid to ask or to learn what you don't know.

It takes some practice and patience to focus on one thing at once and take it step by step, but you will get there. One step at a time. ▪

Gill Fernley

Quick resources:

Success One Step at a Time Visualization: https://www.kathysmith.com/feeling-stuck-get-out-of-a-rut/

Ten-Minute Focus Visualization: https://www.kathysmith.com/10-min-focus-audio-meditation-2/

Music to Write Faster and Better: https://www.youtube.com/watch?v=v3HJYkur4HY

A Rising Tide Lifts All Boats

A RECAP OF THE 20BOOKS VEGAS 2021 CONFERENCE

In November 2021, roughly sixteen hundred authors descended upon Las Vegas to attend the annual 20Booksto50K® conference. Bally's Las Vegas Hotel hosted the event for the first time, the increased number of attendees showcasing the growing popularity of the conference.

It also marked the return of the conference since 2019 after Sam's Town Hotel canceled the 2020 conference due to COVID-19 concerns. For many of the attendees, this was the first time in almost two years that they could meet their friends and peers. For others flying in from Europe and the UK, it was the earliest opportunity to return to the United States—the travel ban had been lifted mere hours earlier. Everyone was eager to learn, reconnect, and network.

You could feel the excitement in the air. Ricardo Fayet, co-founder of Reedsy, said, "It was an incredible feeling to be able to see everyone in person after such a long time. What makes 20BooksVegas special for me is that it brings people in across all genres, levels and opinions while keeping a healthy, supportive, and inspiring spirit for all."

The conference started with an Industry Day where over thirty vendors showcased their products and services, from author programs to website creation and cover design. *Indie Author Magazine* had a table and showcased past issues.

Conference organizer Craig Martelle put together a quality show, arranging an impressive number of sessions and panels. On an average day, attendees had a choice of over forty talks to attend. The speakers included both indie and traditionally published authors, discussing a wide range of topics from craft to marketing. A session was available for authors in each stage of their career in any genre.

Some sessions struck a chord with authors after the turbulent past two years. Tyler Davis mentioned, "I enjoyed both of Becca Syme's panels. They were exactly what I needed after burning myself out in 2020–2021."

David McDowell, a first-time attendee, was impressed by the caliber and generosity of the presenters. "My writing has improved immensely since attending, thanks to the guidance of speakers such as Maxwell Alexander Drake and C.R. Rowenson. Drake's message resonated with me and has guided my writing since. C.R. Rowenson sat with me on his own time to help clarify details of my book that were [eluding] me. The value I gleaned from these two speakers alone was worth the price of admission, and yet I learned so much more."

As one of the presenters at the conference, Monica Leonelle appreciated the myriad paths authors follow to realize their dreams. "The thing that impressed me most about the 20Books conference was how diverse the marketing and sales talks were. There were authors making money from so many different avenues—direct sales, Patreon, Kickstarter, wide retailers, events and signings, and more. For me, the value was in seeing so many people fearlessly forging their own path for their career. People often say the conference is Amazon-centric, and I couldn't disagree more."

Chris Abernathy recollected, "My favorite moment was seeing Sarah Noffke have her moment on stage. It was, to me, exactly what 20Books is about. She was 100 percent celebrating the impact on her life and also 100 percent helping

Ramy Vance believes the value of attending a 20Booksto50K conference is "networking and connecting with other authors."

and inspiring others to overcome their challenges and realize their dreams. And that's not bad math because, with 20Books, the two are the same." Sarah Noffke was on the High Powered Authors panel and spoke about the Production and Writing of a Long Series, both popular sessions with authors lining up to sit in the front row.

Meanwhile, Tao Wong "really enjoyed David Weber's talk about Author Voice. Seeing his own focus on characters helped clarify one option to strengthen my own author voice and the way it can grow in the future."

In addition to regular sessions, genre panels included Post Apocalyptic, Urban Fantasy, Erotica, LitRPG, Action/Adventure, Thriller, Historical, Western, Cozy/Mystery, Space Opera, and Reverse Harem.

In a special setup, authors were invited to pitch their stories to publishers with the aim of securing a publishing deal. Jenn Mitchell participated and revealed, "It was both terrifying (I had to pitch first) and awesome. The publishers were kind and generous with their feedback. The learning experience was invaluable, and it really helped build my confidence as an author."

Jordan Barnes attended the conference after hearing about it from Merri Maywether in a Clubhouse room. He had been part of her regular writing sprint rooms for months, and after attending the conference, he shared, "One highlight for me was when Merri Maywether hosted an impromptu writing sprint after a great day of panels. It was surreal writing with so many friends for the first time in person and sharing the same passion that brought us all together."

But attendees made time for fun too. Since authors love to eat, a popular game during the

In addition to regular sessions, genre panels included Post Apocalyptic, Urban Fantasy, Erotica, LitRPG, Action/ Adventure, Thriller, Historical, Western, Cozy/ Mystery, Space Opera, and Reverse Harem.

week was finding the cake vending machine. Anytime an author discovered it, a photo popped up in the Facebook group. Claire Taylor declared, "My favorite moments at 20Books always take place gathered around food with friends. The magic of it is that you rally a few people you know to grab a bite, but they inevitably bring along people you don't yet know, so you end up sharing every meal with old friends while making a few new ones. That's what in-person gatherings are all about for me."

John Logsdon agreed with Claire's sentiment. "Having meals with fellow authors made for deeper conversations that were enlightening and energizing. Coupled with our spirit-of-sharing 20Books mindset, those side-discussions were invaluable!"

Authors also love to read. Ramy Vance revealed, "One of my favorite moments was meeting an author that I was actually a fan of… I love the Ten Realms series and was at a party when I bumped into a guy named Michael Chatfield. We had a wonderful conversation, and he generously showed me a few things he was working on for the future."

The conference week ended with an author signing event. Dozens of authors participated, and for several authors, the signing event was the first they had attended. Jenn Mitchell acknowledged, "Participating in the Author Signing event was one of the highlights of the show for me. Erika Everest and team did a fabulous job of organizing and executing everything, which made for a smooth and enjoyable experience for the authors."

Not all authors decided to sell their books. Becca Syme disclosed, "I had a table at the signing, and I ended up giving away 100 percent of my books instead of selling them. I always see

"The friendships made during 20books are priceless."
Robyn Wideman

author signing events as an opportunity to get my books in the hands of new readers. I could spend one dollar on a custom piece of swag, or I could spend about one dollar more and send readers away with something they came for—a book. It's promotion for me, just like running ads."

For many authors, the annual 20Booksto50K® Las Vegas conference is not to be missed. Robyn Wideman agreed, "Attending 20books conferences is always a highlight of my year. The opportunity to talk shop... with fellow authors in person is invaluable and always inspirational. The friendships made during 20books are priceless."

Regular attendee and speaker Nora Phoenix lauded the relationship-building available at the conference. "My biggest value was reconnecting with author friends and acquaintances and making new connections... the networking has been so helpful in finding mutual support and encouragement, learning new things, getting opportunities, and having access to information I wouldn't have had otherwise, and so much more."

Post-apocalyptic author and panelist Franklin Horton matched the sentiment. "Aside from the content of the sessions, 20Books offers an unprecedented opportunity to network with your colleagues. For me, this has always been the most significant value of conferences."

Jami Albright said being at the conference fed her soul. "There's something really powerful about being in a room full of people who are all striving for the same things and to be [reminded] that you're not alone on this journey that can be very solitary."

One of the High Powered Authors panelists and presenter of the Rapid Release Marketing talk Elana Johnson affirmed, "My advice is to do what you can to attend the next 20Books confer-

"There are networking opportunities that will take your career to the next level, whether that's through craft or marketing or mindset adjustments."
Elana Johnson

ence in person if at all possible. There is an incredible energy there you can't get anywhere else. There are people you need to meet. There are networking opportunities that will take your career to the next level, whether that's through craft or marketing or mindset adjustments. Attending 20Books in person in 2017 was a key moment for me in realizing that I could take my writing into a full-time business. It was life-changing, and that shift came from being on site and meeting the people already doing it."

R.J. Blain had this advice for people considering attending the next conference. "Unlike most conventions, almost everything is recorded, so when you attend 20Booksto50K®, take care of yourself. You're not going to miss out taking care of yourself during a very long and tiring week. A rested mind learns better!" Virtual attendees could watch sessions live-streamed on Facebook and then transferred to YouTube. You can find most of the sessions here: https://www.youtube.com/c/20Booksto50kRLiveEvents/

Maria Connor summed it up perfectly. "What makes the 20Books conference stand out from other events is its grassroots commitment to supporting all writers through a cohesive, cooperative organization. It strives to make information and resources available to all writers, no matter their goals, level of achievement, genre, experience, or approach to publishing. 20Books participants, organizers, and presenters are knowledgeable, generous, approachable, and committed to helping each and every member level up."

If you have an opportunity to attend in person, do it. If you can't go, the next best thing is to watch all the sessions online. ◼

Fatima Fayez

"There's something really powerful about being in a room full of people who are all striving for the same things and to be [reminded] that you're not alone on this journey that can be very solitary."
Jami Albright

Books We Love

Courtesy of IndieAuthorTools.com
Got a book you love and want to share with us?
Submit a book at IndieAuthorTools.com

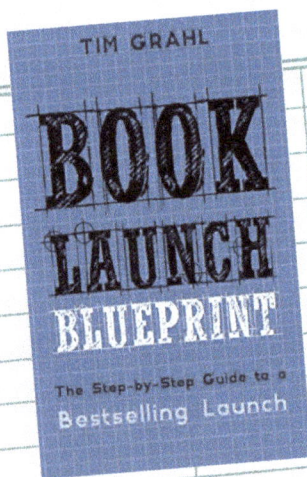

Book Launch Blueprint: The Step-by-Step Guide to a Bestselling Launch

The hardest part of writing a book isn't writing it, it's launching it. Tim Grahl has worked with top best-selling authors such as Hugh Howey, Daniel Pink, Chip and Dan Heath, Sally Hogshead, Michael Bunker, and many more. He's launched dozens of bestselling books, many to the top of the New York Times and Wall Street Journal bestseller lists. In fact, at one point he had 5 clients on the New York Times bestseller list at the same time.

https://www.amazon.com/Book-Launch-Blueprint-Step-Step-ebook/dp/B019JMWGGK/

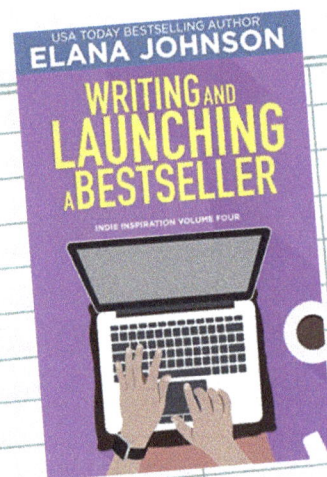

Writing and Launching a Bestseller

Join seven-figure author Elana Johnson as she outlines two of the most important things all self-publishers grapple with: 1. How to write the next bestseller, and 2. How to launch the next bestseller. And bonus - there will be ideas for how to market that new release when it's no longer shiny and fresh.

Writing and launching your next bestseller is only a few steps from where you are right now!

https://www.amazon.com/Writing-Launching-Bestseller-Inspiration-Self-Publishers-ebook/dp/B08R3BPVV3/

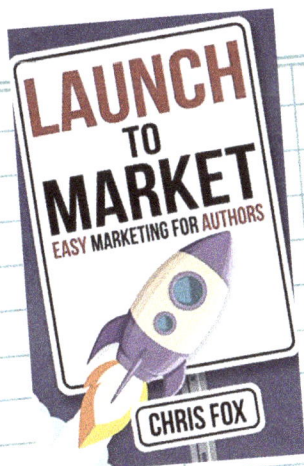

Launch to Market: Easy Marketing For Authors

Launch to Market provides a simple system to plan, track, and execute your book launch. It covers the basics of marketing in an easy to understand way, complete with exercises that will prepare you for your best launch ever. You'll see real sales numbers from an author who just did exactly what you're trying to do, with take aways that will show you exactly how I did it. Don't leave the success of your novel up to chance. Launch your book to market.
https://www.amazon.com/dp/B01FE5C9EA/

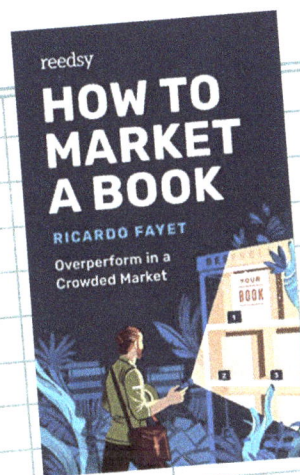

How To Market A Book: Third Edition

How to Market a Book is for authors who want to sell more books, but it's also for those writers who want to think like an entrepreneur and build a long-term income. It's for traditionally published authors who want to take control of their future, and for self-published authors who want to jump-start a career.

There are short-term tactics for those who want to boost immediate sales, but the focus of the book is more about instilling values and marketing principles that will help your long-term career as a writer.
https://www.amazon.com/
How-Market-Book-Third-Writers-ebook/dp/B071NPVK28/

How to Market a Book: Overperform in a Crowded Market (Reedsy Marketing Guides Book 1)

Marketing a book in 2021 can seem like a full-time job, what with the crazy number of things authors seem to be expected to do: social media, blog tours, advertising, price promotions, mailing lists, giveaways, you name it. Instead of drowning you in information or inundating you with hundreds of different tactics and strategies that eventually prove fruitless, this book will guide you through a step-by-step framework to find the ones that actually work for you and your book, so that you can start marketing more efficiently.
https://www.amazon.com/dp/B08TZJQ1FB/

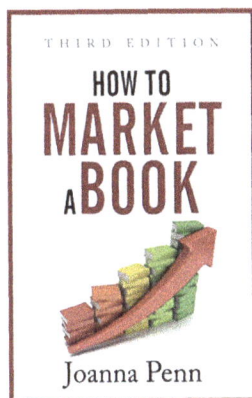

In This Issue

Executive Team

Chelle Honiker, Publisher

As the publisher of Indie Author Magazine, Chelle Honiker brings nearly three decades of startup, technology, training, and executive leadership experience to the role. She's a serial entrepreneur, founding and selling multiple successful companies including a training development company, travel agency, website design and hosting firm, a digital marketing consultancy, and a wedding planning firm. She's organized and curated multiple TEDx events and hired to assist other nonprofit organizations as a fractional executive, including The Travel Institute and The Freelance Association.

As a writer, speaker, and trainer she believes in the power of words and their ability to heal, inspire, incite, and motivate. Her greatest inspiration is her daughters, Kelsea and Cathryn, who tolerate her tendency to run away from home to play with her friends around the world for months at a time. It's said she could run a small country with just the contents of her backpack.

Alice Briggs, Creative Director

As the creative director of Indie Author Magazine, Alice Briggs utilizes her more than three decades of artistic exploration and expression, business startup adventures, and leadership skills. A serial entrepreneur, she has started several successful businesses. She brings her experience in creative direction, magazine layout and design, and graphic design in and outside of the indie author community to her role.

With a masters of science in Occupational Therapy, she has a broad skill set and uses it to assist others in achieving their desired goals. As a writer, teacher, healer, and artist, she loves to see people accomplish all they desire. She's excited to see how IAM will encourage many authors to succeed in whatever way they choose. She hopes to meet many of you in various places around the world once her passport is back in use.

Robyn Sarty, Managing Editor

As a managing editor at Indie Author Magazine, Robyn Sarty brings over a decade of experience as an editor and proofreader. She is the author of two novels and several short stories, and manages her own publishing company. She loves helping other authors with their books and can often be found nerding out over story elements with her friends. She spent five years as a project coordinator for an international engineering firm, and now uses those skills to chase writers instead of engineers and hopes it will be good training for her first marathon.

Growing up as a third culture kid, books were the one constant in her life, and as such, Robyn believes that books are portals to the magic that lies within, and authors are wielders of that magic. She also admits to being a staunch, loyal, and unabashed supporter of the Oxford comma.

Writers

Elaine Bateman

In her pre-author life, Elaine worked for FTSE 100 and Fortune 500 companies in procurement, project support, and IT Training. She has a bachelor of scienceBSc. in Systems Practice and Design.

She is the author of eight published fiction novels and is working on her ninth.

Elaine enjoys giving back to the writing community through her work with 20Booksto50k, an online author community.

She was the Acorn Sports Bar Ladies' Yard-of-Ale Speed-drinking champion of 1985 (she was the only lady to enter and it took her all night.)

She lives in the UK with her husband, son, and three dogs. She no longer drinks ale.

Jackie Dana

Jackie had a few practice careers before finally deciding to become a full-time writer. To keep the computer humming and her cats fed, she's a freelance writer and editor. She's also the brains behind Story Cauldron, a Substack newsletter devoted to storytelling and the writing process as well as the home of her current YA novel series, The Favor Faeries.

Laurel Decher

There might be no frigate like a book, but publishing can feel like a voyage on the H.M.S. Surprise. There's always a twist and there's never a moment to lose.

Laurel's mission is to help you make the most of today's opportunities. She's a strategic problem-solver, tool collector, and co-inventor of the "you never know" theory of publishing.

As an epidemiologist, she studied factors that help babies and toddlers thrive. Now she writes books for children ages nine to twelve about finding more magic in life. She's a member of the Society for Children's Book Writers and Illustrators (SCBWI), has various advanced degrees, and a tendency to smuggle vegetables into storylines.

Fatima Fayez

As a writer for Indie Author Magazine, Fatima unites her love of connecting with people and giving back to the author community. She is a co-founder of The Author Arena podcast, in addition to The Author Conference on Clubhouse. She is also an administrator for the 20BooksTo50K® Facebook group.

Fatima has lived in countries across Europe, Asia, and North America. During her various residencies, she managed to collect a bachelor of science in Journalism, along with a masters in Business Administration, and a handful of management certifications. She currently resides in Kuwait with her family.

On Saturdays, you can find her playing Dungeons & Dragons with her party.

Gill Fernley

Gill Fernley writes fiction in several genres under different pen names, but what all of them have in common is humour and romance, because she can't resist a happy ending or a good laugh. She's also a freelance content writer and has been running her own business since 2013. Before that, she was a technical author and documentation manager for an engineering company and can describe to you more than you'd ever wish to know about airflow and filtration in downflow booths. Still awake? Wow, that's a first! Anyway, that experience taught her how to explain complex things in straightforward language and she hopes it will come in handy for writing articles for IAM. Outside of writing, she's a cake decorator, expert shoe hoarder, and is fluent in English, dry humour and procrastibaking.

Greg R. Fishbone

Greg R. Fishbone is an author of science fiction and mythic fantasy for young readers including the Galaxy Games series of middle grade novels and the mythic fantasy serial, *Becoming Hercules*. Greg is the founder of Mythoversal, a project dedicated to broadening representation in classical tales by amplifying historically marginalized identities and restoring traditions erased by centuries of gatekeeping. As a former Assistant Regional Advisor for the Society of Children's Book Writers and Illustrators, Greg co-directed regional conferences for authors and illustrators and presented workshops on a variety of craft and career development topics. He also served as president of the groundbreaking Class of 2k7 group of debut authors.

Jac Harmon

While studying for her doctorate in Medieval History Jac Harmon spent her time poking around in old buildings and reading manuscripts which gave her plenty of experience when it came to doing the research for her historical fiction. After many years spent working in university administration herding students she is now getting involved in voluntary work at a historic house and being

trained in paper conservation. The idea behind this being that one day she'll be allowed to get her hands on some of the rare books in the library there. Not that this will help with her current novel which is set in the seedy criminal underworld of late-Victorian London. An era of gas lights and grime which was purposefully chosen to give her an excuse to indulge in her love of all things Gothic. Dark twists and bad weather are to be expected.

Kasia Lasinska

Kasia Lasinska holds an LLB in Law with European Legal Studies and an LL.M. in Advanced Studies in International Law. As a practicing attorney, Kasia worked with a top international human rights barrister and then advised clients at a large, international law firm. These inspired her to write dystopian and fantasy novels about corrupt governments and teenagers saving the world.

Kasia has lived in eight countries and speaks five languages (fluently after a glass of wine). She currently lives in London, but her daydreams are filled with beaches and palm trees.

When she's not writing, you can find Kasia scouting out the best coffee shops in town, planning her next great adventure, or petting other people's puppies.

Bre Lockhart

Armed with a degree in Communications and Public Relations, Bre Lockhart survived more than a decade in the corporate America trenches before jumping headfirst into writing urban fantasy and sci-fi, followed later by mystery under a second pen name. She's also one-third of a fiction editing team who probably enjoy their jobs a bit too much most days. As an experienced extrovert, Bre uses her questionable humor and red—sometimes other colors, too—glasses at writer conferences to draw unsuspecting introverts into her bubble of conversation; no one is safe. On her days off, you can find Bre camping and traveling with her family or organizing an expansive collection of lipstick at her home in Tulsa, Oklahoma.

Sìne Màiri MacDougall

Sìne Màiri is a Gàidhlig speaker from the Nova Scotian Gaidhealtachd. She's an author, international incident starter, and recovering educator. Having taught all over the world from the UK to Northern Canada to China, and back again, her specialties are language and literature, history, and youth services for alternative education. She unapologetically writes about the themes she's encountered in her travels; resilience and found family being chief amongst those themes.

Her current fiction projects include two urban fantasy series that she hopes to launch in the coming year.

Merri Maywether

Merri Maywether lives with her husband in rural Montana. You can find her in the town's only coffee house listening to three generations of Montanans share their stories. Otherwise, she's in the classroom or the school library, inspiring the next generation's writers.

Susan Odev

Susan has banked over three decades of work experience in the fields of personal and organizational development, being a freelance corporate trainer and consultant alongside holding down "real" jobs for over twenty-five years. Specializing in entrepreneurial mindsets, she has written several non-fiction business books, once gaining a coveted Amazon #1 best seller tag in business and entrepreneurship, an accolade she now strives to emulate with her fiction.

Currently working on her fifth novel, under a top secret pen name, the craft and marketing aspects of being a successful indie author equally fascinate and terrify her.

A lover of history with a criminal record collection, Susan lives in a retro orange and avocado world. Once described by a colleague as being an "onion," Susan has many layers, as have ogres (according to Shrek). She would like to think this makes her cool, her teenage children just think she's embarrassing.

Nicole Schroeder

Nicole is a storyteller at heart. A journalist, author, and editor from Columbia, Missouri, she delights in any opportunity to shape her own stories or help others do the same. She currently works as a copyeditor for a local newspaper in Washington, Missouri. Before that, she was a reporter and editor for a local arts and culture magazine and last year graduated with a bachelor's degree from the Missouri School of Journalism and minors in English and Spanish. Her creative writing has been published in national literary magazines, and she's helped edit numerous fiction and nonfiction books, including a Holocaust survivor's memoir, alongside international independent publishers. When she's not at her writing desk, Nicole is usually in the saddle, cuddling her guinea pigs, or spending time with family. She loves any excuse to talk about Marvel movies and considers National Novel Writing Month its own holiday.

Emilia Zeeland

Emilia Zeeland is a Young Adult Sci-Fi and Fantasy writer and author of The STAR Academy Series and The Elmwick Academy Series. Even though she holds an international business degree and two Masters, Zeeland's heart is full of love for speculative fiction.

Her own stories include coming-of-age tales, detailed worlds, unimaginable consequences, deep friendships, and romances that sneak up on you. She's not afraid to push her characters to their limits and give them a depth that firmly plants them in readers' hearts. In Zeeland's writing, readers will be transported to another world, where they are not alone, but part of a tightly-knit found family.

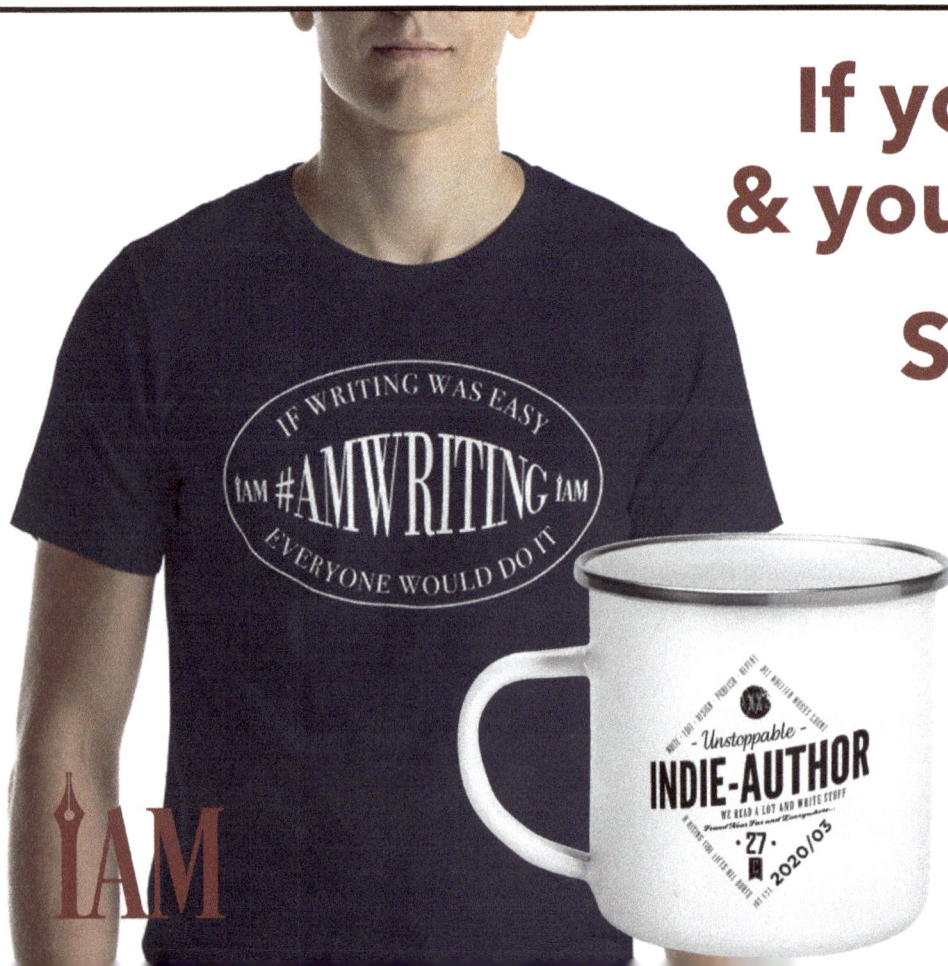

INDIE AUTHOR
NEWS & EVENTS

For the latest on news and events pertinent to the indie author community, please check out our interactive calendar here:

Got news or events to share with the Indie Author Community?
Let us know at
news@indieauthormagazine.com.

Pssssst.....

iAM 's First

AUTHOR
TECH
SUMMIT

May 11-13, 2022

Details to come:

AuthorTechSummit.com